Policy Framework for Investment

2015 Edition

OECD
BETTER POLICIES FOR BETTER LIVES

Please cite this publication as:
OECD (2015), *Policy Framework for Investment 2015 Edition*, OECD Publishing, Paris.
http://dx.doi.org/10.1787/9789264208667-en

ISBN 978-92-64-20865-0 (imprimé)
ISBN 978-92-64-20866-7 (PDF)

Photo credits: © Janne Ahvo/iStock/ThinkStock.com.

Corrigenda to OECD publications may be found on line at: *www.oecd.org/publishing/corrigenda.htm*.

Foreword

The objective of the Policy Framework for Investment *(PFI) is to mobilise private investment that supports steady economic growth and sustainable development, contributing to the economic and social well-being of people around the world. It also aims to advance the implementation of the Sustainable Development Goals and to help mobilise financing for development in support of the post-2015 development agenda.*

Drawing on international good practices, the Framework *proposes guidance in twelve policy fields critically important for improving the quality of a country's enabling environment for investment. It encourages policy makers to ask appropriate questions about their economy, their institutions and their policy settings to identify priorities, to develop an effective set of policies and to evaluate progress.*

The Framework, *initially developed in 2006, was updated by an international task force established under the aegis of the OECD Investment and Development Assistance Committees in the context of the Advisory Group on Investment and Development. The update takes into account feedback from the numerous users of the* Framework *at country and regional levels since its development, as well as changes in the global economic landscape.*

The Framework *was adopted and declassified by the OECD Council, the governing board of the Organisation, and welcomed by Ministers at their annual OECD meeting in June 2015, along with a Recommendation of the Council to promote its use by the international community. The OECD and its partners will continue to work together, in co-operation with the World Bank Group, the United Nations and other interested institutions and with the active engagement of business, labour and other civil society organisations, to support effective use and implementation of the* Framework.

Table of contents

The update of the Policy Framework for Investment

The *Framework* was first developed in 2006 through a task force consisting of officials from some 60 governments. As one of the only policy instruments developed by governments to support international investment policy dialogue, co-operation, and reform, it has been extensively used in dozens of countries in all regions of the world.

This experience has yielded many lessons on how the *Framework* could be improved, particularly to further support the post-2015 development agenda, finding financing for development solutions and implementing the Sustainable Development Goals. Furthermore, the global policy landscape has undergone major changes since it was endorsed at the 2006 OECD Ministerial Council Meeting. New forces have reshaped the investment scene, including the economic and financial crisis which started in 2008, the emergence of new major outward investors, and the spread of global value chains. These prompted OECD Ministers to call for an update of the *Framework*.

The update benefitted from an inclusive multi-stakeholder process, guided by a task force including countries at all levels of development and jointly chaired by Myanmar (Mr. Aung Naing Oo, Director General of the Directorate of Investment and Company Administration of the Ministry of National Planning and Economic Development) and Finland (H.E. Okko-Pekka Salmimies, Ambassador to the OECD and UNESCO), and the OECD Advisory Group on Investment and Development – a joint body of the Investment and Development Assistance Committees.

The World Bank Group, UNCTAD, UNESCAP, the European Commission and other international organisations participated in the update of the *Framework*, including through meetings of the task force and regional consultations in Indonesia, South Africa, Peru, and Sri Lanka. Regional communities such as Asia-Pacific Economic Co-operation, the Association of Southeast Asian Nations, the Southern African Development Community and MENA countries significantly contributed to the update. A Task Force meeting with a focus on implementation was organised jointly with the World Bank Group in Washington, DC. The process greatly benefitted from the inputs received from the Business and Industry Advisory Committee (BIAC), the Trade Union Advisory Committee (TUAC), OECD Watch, other representatives from business, non-governmental organisations and think tanks at numerous public consultations, as well as an online consultation process.

In addition to the Investment Committee and the Development Assistance Committee, thirteen other OECD bodies were involved in the update of the *Framework*: the Working Party on Responsible Business Conduct; the Working Party of the Trade Committee; the Working Party on Climate, Investment and Development; the Public Governance Committee; the Regulatory Policy Committee; the Working Party on Tax Policy; the Committee on Fiscal Affairs; the Corporate Governance Committee; the Employment, Labour and Social Affairs

Committee; the Competition Committee; the Working Party on SMEs and Entrepreneurship; the Committee on Financial Markets; and the Insurance and Private Pensions Committee.

In the OECD Secretariat, the update was managed by the Investment Division with contributions from the Competition, Anti-Corruption, Corporate Affairs, and Financial Affairs Divisions of the Directorate for Enterprise and Financial Affairs. Significant inputs were provided by the Development Co-operation Directorate; the Centre for Tax Policy and Administration; the Tax and Development Programme; the Environment Directorate; the Directorate for Science, Technology and Innovation; the Trade and Agriculture Directorate; the Directorate for Employment, Labour and Social Affairs; the Directorate on Public Governance and Territorial Development; the Centre for Entrepreneurship, SMEs and Local Development; and the Global Relations Secretariat.

Preamble

The objective of the *Policy Framework for Investment* is to mobilise private investment that supports steady economic growth and sustainable development, contributing to the economic and social well-being of people around the world.

The *Framework* is a tool, providing a checklist of key policy issues for consideration by any government interested in creating an enabling environment for all types of investment and in enhancing the development benefits of investment to society. In this way, the *Framework* also aims to advance the implementation of the Sustainable Development Goals and to help mobilise financing for development.

The *Framework* should be seen in the broad context of recent global efforts to strengthen the international and national environments in which economic activity is conducted. In common with those initiatives, it promotes transparency and appropriate roles and responsibilities for governments, business, civil society and others with a stake in promoting development and poverty reduction and builds on shared values of democratic society and respect for human rights.

The core purpose of the *Framework* is to encourage policy makers to ask appropriate questions about their economy, their institutions and their policy settings in order to identify priorities, to develop an effective set of policies and to evaluate progress. It is not a volume of ready-made prescriptions, nor is it binding. Rather, it is a flexible tool with which to frame and evaluate the important policy challenges countries face in pursuit of development through investment.

In 2006, a task force of government officials from 60 OECD and non-OECD economies developed the *Framework's* content and structure through regional consultations in Africa, Asia, Latin America and South East Europe. The World Bank, the United Nations and other international institutions, as well as business, labour and civil society organisations also contributed the development of the *Framework*.

Since its development, the *Framework* has been used world-wide for country-level OECD *Investment Policy Reviews*, sub-national level applications, numerous regional investment programmes and dialogues, and within regional groupings, such as the Association of Southeast Asian Nations and the Southern African Development Community, as well as in the context of the G20. It has also been used extensively for targeted capacity building activities, peer reviews and knowledge sharing, and technical advisory work on investment and development. Sectoral applications of the *Framework* have also been developed, such as the *Policy Framework for Investment in Agriculture* and the *Policy Guidance for Investment in Clean Energy Infrastructure*.

To take this experience and the changes in the global economic landscape into account, the update of the *Framework* was carried out in 2014-15 under a task force co-chaired by Myanmar and Finland. The update also benefitted from the contribution of the OECD

Advisory Group on Investment and Development, and various public consultations, online dialogues and seminars.

The updated *Framework* is comprehensive but does not claim to be exhaustive. Beyond macroeconomic stability, political predictability, social cohesion and upholding the rule of law, which are pre-conditions for sustainable development, the *Framework* considers numerous policy dimensions in an integrated manner, drawing on global good practices including: investment policy; investment promotion and facilitation; trade policy; competition policy; tax policy; public governance; corporate governance; policies for enabling responsible business conduct; human resources development; an investment framework for green growth; private investment in infrastructure; and financing for investment. The *Framework* helps governments consider these policy areas as a whole, supporting policy coherence in support of economic, social, and environmental goals.

Other policy areas, such as rural development, the promotion of small and medium-sized enterprises, innovation, gender balance and entrepreneurship bear on the business environment as well. While the *Framework* does not identify these topics as stand-alone sections, it explicitly captures their importance on the investment environment and for sustainable development through specific questions in different policy sections.

The *Framework,* by fostering an informed process of policy formulation and implementation at all levels of government, can be used in a variety of ways as part of national and regional development strategies. Self-evaluation, peer reviews, regional co-operation and multilateral discussions can all benefit from the insights offered in the *Framework* and contribute to identifying where to prioritise investment policy reforms for sustainable development. The *Framework* also provides a reference point for international organisations' capacity building programmes, for investment promotion agencies, and for donors as they assist developing country partners in improving the investment environment. It also supports business, labour and other non-governmental organisations in their dialogue with governments. As evidenced through its application since 2006, the *Framework* can be flexibly adapted to the particular economic, social, legal and cultural circumstances and needs in economies at different stages of development. It can also serve as a basis for international co-operation on investment-related issues, including through regional and home-country policy initiatives.

The OECD, working with Member and non-Member economies, partner organisations, donors and stakeholders, will assist in developing methodologies, including indicators of progress, and institutional capacity building for the effective use of the *Framework* in light of different circumstances and needs. The *Framework* also builds on the OECD's experience and instruments dealing with the different policy areas that are covered and its Committees' global and regional dialogue with non-member economies. It complements recent OECD initiatives directed to governments and the business sector, including the OECD *Guidelines for Multinational Enterprises* updated in 2011, and can work in synergy with the OECD Development Assistance Committee's work on leveraging private sector-led sustainable growth.

Introduction

The *Policy Framework for Investment* addresses the issue of sustainable and inclusive development through the lens of private sector-led development. An investment climate focus provides a coherent and comprehensive way of addressing the challenges of growth and development, one which looks at the issue at a micro level from the viewpoint of the principal agent for productivity improvements: the firm. This focus is not meant to accord primacy to the concerns of private investors; private and social returns from investment are not always congruous, and governments appropriately have a broader development agenda than corporate profitability. But it does provide a framework for understanding how policies interact and affect outcomes, while also bringing out the critical importance of public governance.

The *Framework* looks at all forms of investment involving all types of firms. A good investment climate is one which provides opportunities for all investors: public and private, large and small, and foreign and domestic. The heterogeneity of investors, the diversity of factors which drive investment decisions and the multiple policy objectives pursued by governments all call for a whole-of-government perspective so as to increase policy coherence. This policy coherence applies to each component of the investment climate, whether encouraging foreign investment, promoting linkages and technology spillovers, raising the quality of the workforce, improving infrastructure or any other area.

The *Framework* is non-prescriptive; there is no one-size-fits-all approach to private sector development that will work in all countries in all sectors and at all times. It recognises the role of competition in stimulating productivity growth and the related principle of non-discrimination and national treatment, but it also recognises the economic efficiency is only one part of the equation.

Public governance matters as much as policies for the investment climate. The *Framework* considers not just policies themselves but also how they are developed, co-ordinated, implemented, evaluated and ultimately modified. Investment involves a judgement about the future. What matters for investors are all the principles embodied in the notion of the rule of law: predictability, transparency, credibility, accountability and fairness. The *Framework* was created in response to this complexity, fostering a flexible, whole-of-government approach which recognises that investment climate improvements require not just policy reform but also changes in the way governments go about their business.

Investment for growth and development

Investment is central to growth and sustainable development. It expands an economy's productive capacity and drives job creation and income growth. Most investment is undertaken by domestic firms, but international investment can provide additional advantages beyond its contribution to the capital stock. It can serve as a conduit for the local diffusion of technology and expertise such as through the creation of local supplier linkages and by providing improved access to international markets.

The *Framework* interprets investment in its broadest sense. Investment can take many forms, from physical assets to human or intellectual capital. It can add capacity or simply improve the efficiency of existing assets such as through a change of ownership. Under the right conditions, it raises overall output both through factor accumulation and by introducing new techniques and processes which boost productivity and ultimately the country's standard of living.

Investment should not be seen as an end in itself. Indeed, some sectors and economies at certain points in time may suffer from a surfeit of investment, resulting in excess capacity and wasted resources. Investment might also flow into sectors which do not provide sufficient productive or social benefits or which cause environmental degradation. The growth and development impact of investment will depend as much if not more on the quality of the investment as it does on the quantity.

Like the notion of investment, the concept of the climate for investment should be interpreted broadly. A good investment climate helps to mobilise capital, skills, technology and intermediate inputs to allow firms to expand. It helps to channel resources to more productive uses, and, through competitive pressure and the discipline imposed by shareholders and creditors, ensures that all firms strive to improve their efficiency and allows inefficient ones to exit. It should allow enterprises to invest productively and profitably, but it is not just about reducing the cost of doing business and raising corporate profitability. It should also ensure that investment brings about the highest possible economic and social impact.

The *Framework* includes the key policy areas contributing to a healthy investment climate that meets the needs of both investors and of society more broadly. Each set of policies influences investors' decisions and the social and economic returns through several channels. To understand why these policy areas were selected and how they interact with the investment climate requires an understanding of how investment contributes to growth and raises living standards through productivity improvements.

Why do we care about productivity?

Productivity growth is essential for long-term improvements in the standard of living. Achieving the efficiency improvements – both within sectors and within firms – necessary for such growth is a challenge for all countries, whether developing or more advanced. In the early stages of development, productivity will rise as workers shift out of sectors such as subsistence agriculture towards more productive activities in manufacturing. Ultimately, however, productivity growth will stem from efficiency improvements within sectors, as the most efficient competitors gain market share at the expense of those lagging behind (allocative efficiency) and as competition pushes all remaining firms in the sector to improve their performance (firm-level efficiency).

Achieving these productivity gains involves many areas of the *Framework*. Reforms in one area that do not address systemic obstacles more broadly may not achieve their desired impact on efficiency.

- *Allocative efficiency* requires: well-functioning capital markets; labour regulations which, while protecting workers' rights and respecting internationally recognised labour standards, do not impede necessary corporate restructuring; bankruptcy laws; competition policy to ensure that incumbent firms, including sometimes state-owned enterprises, do not restrict new market entry, and investment policy and promotion to provide access and assistance for foreign investment.

- *Firm-level efficiency* improvements come primarily from competition. Without the pressure of market entry, firms have less incentive to innovate and improve their efficiency. Empirical studies find that industries with more competition experience faster productivity growth. Competition can come from domestic and international rivals, whether exporting to the market or investing directly. Competition policy plays a central role in making markets contestable and hence in ensuring productive outcomes.

Firms also become more competitive by having more and better quality inputs at their disposal, such as capital, skilled or specialised labour, technology and infrastructure. These issues are covered throughout the *Framework*. Technological diffusion, for example, is one way in which firms acquire technological knowledge, learning new and better ways of doing things. This will depend on opportunities to develop domestic technological capabilities and to absorb foreign technologies through imports and foreign direct investment (FDI), the capacity of local firms and workers to absorb this knowledge through linkages, the willingness of foreign firms to share this knowledge given adequate intellectual property rights protection and the ability to maintain full control of the affiliate.

More efficient and effective government

Underpinning these efficiency gains at the level of the firm is an effective and efficient system of public governance, including above all respect for the rule of law. Some elements of what is commonly meant by the rule of law are provided in Box 1. The *Framework* addresses the quality of public institutions and the capacity of the civil service and considers how laws are made and implemented, including the whole policy cycle of design, consultation, implementation, evaluation and review.

Box 1. **Elements of the rule of law**

1. The law must be accessible, intelligible and predictable.
2. Questions of legal right and liability should ordinarily be resolved by application of the law and not the exercise of discretion.
3. The law should apply equally to all, unless objective, clearly stated differences justify discrimination.
4. Ministers, officers of the courts and public officers at all levels must exercise the powers conferred on them in good faith, fairly, for the purpose for which the powers were conferred, without exceeding the limits of such powers and not unreasonably.
5. The law must afford adequate protection of fundamental human rights, as well as property rights.
6. Adjudicative procedures provided by the state should be fair and conducted without prohibitive cost or inordinate delay.
7. The state should comply with its obligations in international law as in national law.

Source: Adapted from Bingham, T. (2010), *The Rule of Law*, Penguin Books.

One manifestation of poor governance is a high administrative burden on investors which adds to the cost of doing business while also hampering the efficiency and effectiveness of public administration itself. Excessive regulations can be a major cost for investors, particularly for small and medium-sized enterprises (SMEs), and can help to explain the high incidence of informality in an economy or a poor performance in attracting FDI.

The *Framework* recognises a government's right to regulate in the public interest to achieve established policy objectives and does not assume that less regulation is always better. Well-crafted regulations can improve the investment climate by creating an efficient framework and ensuring high standards of rule of law. Good regulation does not necessarily mean less regulation. Rather, it suggests that administrative burdens should be streamlined where necessary and that the objectives of regulations should be transparent and their effectiveness regularly monitored and evaluated.

Costs of doing business

Many policy areas of the *Framework* consider the costs of doing business in the economy. For a potential investor, these must be judged against the expected returns from the investment and, for export-oriented projects, the costs in alternate locations. These include the following costs:

- capital (debt and equity);
- labour (skilled and unskilled, adjusted for productivity);
- intermediate inputs (both local and imported);
- infrastructure (transport, telecoms, energy, etc.);
- land;
- administrative (complying with regulations);
- taxation;
- corruption; and
- information and search costs.

The *Framework* looks at how to increase access to finance, how to ensure that labour markets provide workers with the skills required by investors, how trade policies which facilitate access to imports of intermediate inputs can improve competitiveness in export markets, and how to channel investment into infrastructure sectors. Concerning administrative costs and corporate taxation, the *Framework* focuses on how to make the system more efficient. It also looks at how to address the scourge of corruption, which can be a significant operating cost in some markets. The investment promotion section also addresses information costs for investors seeking suitable investment opportunities and local suppliers.

Coping with risk

Investment implies a commitment of resources in the present for an uncertain return in the future. While commercial risk is a natural part of doing business, unforeseen policy changes can also have major implications for the viability of a project. Policy predictability is one of the most commonly cited concerns of investors in surveys.

Regulatory risk can be mitigated by governments by providing greater certainty for investors through transparency and consultations when policy reforms are undertaken and in the way any potential disputes handled. Investors care about regulatory risks. They are anticipated through higher hurdle rates for a project and translate into lower efficiency even if the investment goes ahead because of high expected returns.

One way to enhance policy predictability is to ensure that potential changes involve substantial public consultations in the drafting phase, with the private sector, workers' organisations, as well as other stakeholders. An economy where the rule of law is firmly upheld will also reassure potential investors that any disputes that may arise, whether with commercial partners or with the government, will be handled fairly, with full respect for the rights of the investor.

Governments can also provide, through bilateral investment treaties or on a case-by-case basis, recourse to other means of dispute resolution. If the government chooses to ratify investment treaties, complementary measures must be taken to raise awareness across government of the commitments undertaken, to build capacity within government to implement these commitments and to develop mechanisms (such as an investment ombudsman) to help prevent disputes from arising.

Non-discrimination

The discussion of the rule of law is partly one of whether all economic actors – both in government and the private sector – are equal under the law. But in many cases, the laws themselves favour some investors over others. This discrimination can be between foreign and domestic, public and private, large and small, incumbent and new entrants, or even within a firm between different categories of shareholders.

Almost all governments discriminate in one way or another, sometimes deliberately, sometimes unwittingly. Foreign investors, for example, sometimes face restrictions on their ownership in a local company, particularly in key sectors. Sometimes state-owned enterprises are exempt from competition law and SMEs might also benefit from favourable treatment, whether fiscal advantages or regulatory exemptions. Productivity losses can arise not only in the sector itself but also in downstream sectors dependent upon inputs from the protected sector.

The *Framework* addresses the issue of discrimination in many policy areas, pointing out the potential costs in terms of forgone investment and efficiency gains, but without questioning the right of governments to favour some investors over others in order to achieve other social, economic or environmental goals. Governments may nevertheless wish to consider whether non-discriminatory measures would be adequate to address specific concerns. When discriminatory policies are necessary, they should be proportional – not greater than needed to address broader concerns – and set against measurable objectives and regularly assessed against those objectives. Regular evaluations can be encouraged by requiring periodic renewal of the discriminatory restrictions.

The private sector is diverse

The discussion of discrimination brings to the fore the notion that there is not one investment climate in an economy but several. Not only do some firms face more restrictions than others, but different firms in different sectors are not affected in the same way or to the same extent by the costs and risks described earlier. Some policy areas matter more for some investors than for others. An attractive investment climate takes into account this heterogeneity of firms in an economy: public and private, foreign and domestic, large and small and also formal and informal.

Even for similar firms, the policy environment may differ strongly depending on the location of the activity, with special economic zones for example providing an environment with fewer of the regulatory hurdles and other obstacles found in the rest of the economy. The policy environment may also differ significantly by sector and by province.

Even when firms face exactly the same regulations, implementation can vary tremendously. As a result, variations in the ease of doing business within an economy can sometimes be as great as those across countries. Firms facing the fewest obstacles in terms of implementation are likely to be large and well-connected local companies or investors in priority sectors. Differential de facto treatment can be as much an impediment to productivity growth and to a good investment climate more generally as statutory discrimination.

Promoting responsible investment

Sustainability and responsible investment are integral parts of a good investment climate and should be factored in from the beginning and not as an after-thought. Principles related to the rule of law in Box 1, if well implemented, will help to ensure that firms act responsibly, by setting out what is expected of them and by making clear the sanction in the event of a breach in these expectations. Governments can also sign on to international standards, such as the OECD *Guidelines for Multinational Enterprises,* or create a focal point for responsible business conduct within the government to assist in ensuring that foreign investors in its territory and its own firms investing abroad act responsibly.

In some situations, such as post-conflict contexts, governments may not only lag behind international expectations concerning laws ensuring responsible behaviour by investors, but they may also lack the administrative capacity to implement these standards in the first place.

Responsibility is not just a consideration for foreign investors keen to preserve their international reputation. It now affects all enterprises participating in supply chains, whether foreign or domestically-owned. An investment climate that does not include respect for certain rules of responsible business conduct, including relating to accepted international labour and environmental standards, risks being shunned by international investors and by foreign customers.

Getting investment to where it is needed

Much of the discussion so far has been about removing unnecessary impediments to investment within the economy. But ensuring inclusive and sustainable development sometimes means channelling investment into particular sectors or activities. This might involve support for small, family-owned firms or those activities that support greater gender equity in the workforce. It might be sector-specific such as infrastructure or to promote green growth: investment in green infrastructure, sustainable resource management or encouragement of the environmental goods and services sector.

Part of this effort to channel investment will involve removing sector-specific impediments, whether policy-induced or specific to the market structure of each sector. This effort might be complemented by targeted and well-designed incentives, but more broadly, it will also require policies to ensure that returns to investors in that sector are sufficient to entice them to invest.

Horizontal policies and practices

An effective investment policy is grounded in strong institutions and effective public governance. The key pre-requisites for investment policy include respect for the rule of law, quality regulation, transparency and openness and integrity. Effective action across these dimensions will encourage investment and reduce the costs of doing business. Strong institutions help to maintain a predictable and transparent environment for investors.

Investment policy is facilitated by an environment of trust. High levels of trust can facilitate compliance with laws and regulations, strengthen investor confidence and reduce risk aversion. On average only 40% of OECD citizens report that they trust their government, while 57% feel that corruption is widespread in business (Gallup World Poll, 2013). This also reflects the legacy of the crisis, which stemmed from numerous regulatory failures and mismanagement not only by government but also by business, which had implications for trust. Regaining public trust will require governments to demonstrate that they are capable and reliable lawmakers and regulators, and that their decisions are fair and free from undue influence. Underlying trust is the expectation that public officials respect high standards of integrity; in particular that issues of conflict of interest are addressed rigorously, that lobbying guidelines are respected and that corruption and fraud in high-risk areas such as public procurement are effectively addressed.

Whole-of-government approaches to investment policy will improve outcomes and enhance the use of public resources. Investment policy – like competitiveness, climate change mitigation, managing demographic change and innovation – is an issue requiring policy responses that do not fit neatly within any single governmental department or agency. Investors increasingly expect public policies and services to be seamless and responsive to their needs, not defined by siloed administrative structures. Good government is now about joint action, where administrations work in a co-ordinated and collaborative manner across boundaries. Poor co-ordination can increase the risk of duplication, inefficient spending, lower-quality service, and contradictory objectives and targets, all of which can undermine investor confidence. "Whole-of-government" approaches to policy design and delivery are becoming a common objective for many public administrations as a way to integrate cross-disciplinary perspectives into policy, improve co-ordination, and facilitate resource sharing and have to be accompanied by single windows facilitating the investor interface with government. Investment policies, which have multiple objectives and involve many economic actors, from SMEs to multinationals, are a prime example of the need for a whole-of-government approach. Coherence is particularly important in regulation, which is one of the main pillars of an effective investment policy.

Inter-governmental coordination. Overlapping and sometimes conflicting rules, procedures and regulations across ministries and levels of government, including between the central and provincial levels and sometimes between supranational and national authorities can create administrative burdens on investors. Different countries will opt for different degrees of decentralisation, but OECD country experience suggests that some central coordination is essential for successful regulatory governance.

Transparency and engagement can deliver better policies with more stakeholder support. Transparency is an essential component of good governance today. More open and inclusive policy-making processes help to ensure that policies will better match the needs and expectations of citizens and businesses. Greater participation of stakeholders in policy design and implementation leads to better targeted and more effective policies. The notion of "open government" is rapidly transforming the way public institutions work, both internally and with citizens, businesses and workers' organisations. Soliciting investor views, along with those of other stakeholders, when developing or revising policies contributes to policy legitimacy and effectiveness. Moreover, policy is more likely to be sound and not produce unintended side effects if it is formed in a structured and transparent way that gathers input from all interested parties.

Innovation and improvement in policy design and delivery. The shift to open government provides an important incentive for the public administration to enhance its performance. Businesses, investors and citizens are all more able to assess the outcomes of public policy, comment on failures and poor performance and challenge the government to improve. Over time, this is becoming an important force for reform and modernisation in service delivery, making the most of new information and communication technologies. Non-government stakeholders are increasingly involved in designing and implementing policy, and even monitoring progress. Through websites, user-friendly data and information tools, governments can engage diverse actors in public policy implementation and evaluation. Investment policies should also benefit from innovative approaches across the policy cycle.

International co-operation can complement and even reinforce domestic efforts to improve the business climate. The more standards are harmonised or mutually recognised across countries, the more easily will firms be able to invest and trade internationally. International trade and investment agreements can provide added transparency concerning the regulation of foreign investors in signatory countries.

Core questions and principles

1. Are laws and regulations and their implementation and enforcement clear, transparent and readily accessible? Does this transparency cover procedural issues as well?
2. How does the government ensure that laws and regulations do not impose an unnecessary burden on investors? Is there a built-in mechanism to periodically review these burdens? Are these burdens measured and quantified?
3. How does the government ensure a sufficient degree of policy predictability for investors? Is there a review process for administrative decisions?
4. Has the government established effective public consultation mechanisms and procedures, including prior notification requirements, before enacting new laws and regulations?
5. In the exercise of its right to regulate and to deliver public services, does the government have mechanisms in place to ensure transparency of any discrimination against any group of investors and to periodically review their costs against the intended public purpose?
6. What mechanisms exist to manage and co-ordinate regulatory policy across different levels of government to ensure consistency and a transparent application of regulations?

Supplemental questions

Transparency	• How does the government promote awareness of the importance of transparency within government? • Are there legal requirements for transparency? Do they apply to both primary and secondary legislation? At both national and sub-national levels? • Does transparency also extend to rulings and judicial decisions? • How are laws and regulations made readily available, or available upon request, to foreign investors? Are English or other foreign language translations of laws readily available? Do investment promotion agencies play a role in this regard? • How are the special difficulties of SMEs in obtaining information addressed? • Are exceptions to transparency, based on e.g. national security or confidentiality, clearly defined and delimited? • Are the criteria for the exercise of discretion by the procurement authorities clearly articulated and accessible to the public? • Is there a register of existing and proposed regulations? • Is regulatory material disseminated electronically?
Public consultation	• Are stakeholders normally notified and consulted in advance of the purpose and nature of regulatory changes of interest to them? What are the main avenues? Are notice and comment procedures codified? • Are opportunities for public consultation well-publicised, well-organised, highly accessible and well-timed? • Do consultations allow sufficient access for all interested parties, including SMEs, workers' organisations, and foreign investors? • Is there clear guidance to regulators on how consultations should be conducted? • Are other levels of government and line ministries also consulted?
Policy stability and predictability	• What does the government do to enhance policy stability and predictability? • Are the interests of existing investors taken into account when regulations are amended? • See also Sections 1 and 3 on international investment and trade agreements.
Periodic evaluation and review	• Are policies reviewed periodically to see whether they have achieved their objectives? • Are alternatives considered to achieve the same objectives? • Are regulatory impact assessments required for new or amended laws? Are RIAs used to review the existing stock of legislation?

Additional resources

Principles, standards

APEC-OECD (2005), *APEC-OECD Integrated Checklist on Regulatory Reform*, OECD and Asia-Pacific Economic Co-operation, *www.oecd.org/regreform/34989455.pdf*.

OECD Framework for Investment Policy Transparency, OECD Publishing, Paris, *www.oecd.org/investment/investment-policy/16793978.pdf*.

OECD (2003), *Public Sector Transparency and the International Investor*, OECD Publishing, Paris, *www.oecd.org/investment/investment-policy/18546790.pdf*.

OECD Reference Checklist for Regulatory Decision-Making, OECD Publishing, Paris, *www.oecd.org/regreform/regulatory-policy/35220214.pdf*.

Tools, guidance, manuals

OECD (2003), *Open Government: Fostering Dialogue with Civil Society*, OECD Publishing, Paris, *http://dx.doi.org/10.1787/9789264019959-en*.

OECD (2013), *Government at a Glance 2013*, OECD Publishing, Paris, *http://dx.doi.org/10.1787/gov_glance-2013-en*.

OECD (2001), *Citizens as Partners: OECD Handbook on Information, Consultation and Public participation in Policy-Making*, OECD Publishing, Paris, *http://dx.doi.org/10.1787/9789264195578-en*.

European Commission (2005), *Consultation with stakeholders in the shaping of national and regional policies affecting small business, Final Report of the Expert Group*, Best Procedure Project, European Commission, Brussels, *http://ec.europa.eu/DocsRoom/documents/2114/attachments/1/translations/en/renditions/native*.

World Bank (2006), *Business licensing reform: a toolkit for development practitioners*, World Bank, Washington, DC.

Indicators, benchmarking

World Bank, Ease of Doing Business Indicators, *www.doingbusiness.org/*.

World Bank, Worldwide Governance Indicators, *http://info.worldbank.org/governance/wgi/index.aspx#home*.

Policy Framework for Investment
2015 Edition

1. Investment policy

The concept of investment policy is interpreted broadly in the *Policy Framework for Investment*. It refers not only to laws, regulations and policies relating to the admission of investors, the rules once established and the protection of their property, but also to the goals and expectations concerning the contribution of investment to sustainable development, such as those outlined in national development plans. As in other areas of the *Framework*, the way that investment policy is developed and modified influences investment decisions. Investment is by nature forward looking, and the transparency, predictability and credibility of policies are important considerations. Policies by their nature change over time; what matters most for investors is how these changes are undertaken, as explained below.

Investment policy is sometimes embodied in a stand-alone investment law, sometimes covering both foreign and domestic investors, sometimes involving two separate laws. It can address both the degree of openness to investment and the protection offered to investors and often includes a list of sectors where investors face restrictions, whether in the law itself or in its implementing regulations. This so-called negative list can include sub-sectors or sectors where all private investment is prohibited or restricted, sectors reserved to small and medium-sized enterprises (SMEs), or those where foreign investors face restrictions. By increasing transparency and predictability, an investment law may also serve as a signalling device and hence help to promote the country as an investment destination.

Many countries, including OECD Members, do not have a specific investment law. Such a law is neither a guarantee of, nor a prerequisite for, a sound investment policy framework. Investment policy can be embodied in other legislation (e.g. the Constitution, laws regulating the behaviour of companies or sector-specific legislation). While an investment law may add transparency to the applicable investment regime, it can also create uncertainty if inconsistent with other laws. International investment agreements, discussed separately at the end of this section, add a layer to a country's investment policy, by providing complementary protections to foreign investors covered by the treaties.

Transparency and predictability

A fair, transparent, clear and predictable regulatory framework for investment is a critical determinant of investment decisions and their contribution to development. It is especially important for SMEs that tend to face particular challenges to entering, and abiding by the rules of, the formal economy. It is also important for foreign investors who may have to function with very different regulatory systems, cultures and administrative frameworks from their own. Uncertainty about the enforceability of lawful rights and obligations raises the cost of capital, thereby weakening firms' competitiveness and reducing investment. Moreover, such ambiguity in the legal system can also foster corruption: investors may be more likely to seek to protect or advance their interests through bribery and government actors may seek undue benefits.

Governments can enhance the quality of the regulatory framework for investment by: consulting with interested stakeholders; simplifying and codifying legislation, including sector-specific legislation; drafting in clear language; developing registers of existing and proposed regulations; expanding the use of electronic dissemination of regulatory material; and by publishing and reviewing administrative decisions. Effective implementation of the regulatory framework for investment can also be improved by ensuring that officials responsible for applying regulations have adequate credentials, are well-trained, provided with fair salaries, and have sufficient resources for carrying out their tasks. Officials should be fully accountable for their actions, particularly those involving discretionary decision-making.

The components of domestic investment policy

The non-discrimination principle, the degree of openness to foreign investment, the protection of investors' property rights and mechanisms for settling investment disputes are core investment policy issues that underpin efforts to create a quality investment environment for all.

Non-discrimination

Non-discrimination is a central tenet of an attractive investment climate. The non-discrimination principle provides that all investors in like circumstances are treated equally, irrespective of their ownership. It can feature as a general principle in the Constitution or at lower regulatory levels, such as in the investment law, and may vary greatly in its scope of application. One of the concepts derived from the principle of non-discrimination in the context of foreign investment is that of national treatment, which requires that a government treat foreign-owned or -controlled enterprises no less favourably than domestic enterprises in like situations.

No government applies national treatment across the board, even in OECD Member countries where restrictions on foreign investment tend, on average, to be lower than in other parts of the world. If other attributes of the investment climate are favourable, investors may still come even if they face some operational restrictions once established, although restrictions on foreign direct investment (FDI) have been found to result in less FDI overall. Beyond the impact on FDI, any policy that favours some firms over others involves a cost, notably less competition and hence lower firm-level efficiency. For this reason, exceptions to non-discrimination need to be evaluated with a view to determining whether the original motivation behind an exception (e.g. protection based on the infant industry argument) remains valid, supported by an evaluation of the costs and benefits, including an assessment of the proportionality of the measure. Broad consideration of the costs and benefits is especially important in service sectors that support a wide range of economic activities across the economy.

Exceptions to national treatment are often enshrined in a negative list attached to the investment law. In the absence of such a list, foreign investors must look to sectoral legislation for guidance. The main types of restrictions faced by foreign investors are listed below:

- Approval mechanisms for foreign investors
- Foreign equity limits

- Key personnel (foreign managers, technical experts and board members)
- Profit and capital repatriation
- Land ownership for business purposes
- Branching limitations
- Reciprocity requirements
- Minimum capital requirements different from those for local companies
- Local content requirements
- Access to local finance
- Government procurement favouring locally-owned over foreign-established companies

Potential discrimination between foreign and domestic investors can work both ways. Foreign investors may receive incentives that are not available to domestic investors. Policy options to manage incentives responsibly are discussed in subsequent sections of the *Framework*.

Protection of property rights

Expropriation

The concept of expropriation includes *direct expropriation* where the state obtains a formal transfer of title or outright physical seizure and *indirect expropriation* where a state interferes in the use of a property or in the enjoyment of its benefits even where the property is not seized and the legal title to the property is not affected. The degree of protection against indirect expropriation under domestic laws varies significantly across countries, including OECD members. Determining whether a regulation may constitute an indirect expropriation for which compensation should be paid is made on a case-by-case basis. It is not enough that a regulation adversely affects profits for it automatically to be regarded as an act of expropriation. Some legislation provides that, except in rare circumstances, non-discriminatory regulatory actions to protect legitimate public welfare objectives, such as public health, safety and the environment, are not considered to constitute expropriation.

Securing land tenure

Secure and well-defined land rights encourage new investments and the upkeep of existing investments as well as sustainable land management. Investors need to be confident that their land rights are properly recognised and protected and that they are protected against forced evictions without compensation. Tenure security does not necessarily require private ownership or a formal title. Simple land use rights, such as lease rights, can provide tenure security if they are clear, of specific duration and the contract cannot be unilaterally broken. Tenure security is not so much derived from the legal status of the rights held, as from social consensus on the legitimacy of these rights and the reliability of mechanisms for settling disputes should they arise.

In order to provide for secure land tenure rights, the land administration should be accessible, reliable and transparent. The responsibilities of the central government versus local authorities should be clearly defined to promote efficiency, reduce corruption, and enhance law implementation and enforcement. If accompanied by appropriate capacity-building and financing mechanisms at the local level, the decentralisation of land rights allocation and administration can ensure higher accountability in land management and facilitate the involvement of local communities in the decision-making process.

The land administration should actively contribute to land use planning in order to ensure sustainable investment and balanced territorial development and help reconcile the different objectives of land use. Land use plans should be developed at all government levels and updated regularly through wide public participation to minimise the risks of land disputes and to ensure that the priorities and interests of local communities are reflected. They should take into account the multifaceted economic, social, cultural, environmental and political roles played by land.

If properly undertaken, land rights registration can enhance land tenure security by recording individual and collective land tenure rights, thereby facilitating the transfer of land tenure rights and allowing investors to seek legal redress in cases of violation of their tenure rights. Land titles can allow land rights holders to use land as collateral to access credit. Land registers and land information systems should be properly maintained and publicised. Comprehensive and up-to-date land registers can cut the time to acquire land tenure rights, reduce corruption and facilitate tax collection. If not properly maintained, land registers can actually increase the likelihood of land disputes.

Acquiring land tenure rights is often a complex and slow process for large investors and measures to facilitate land acquisition can effectively facilitate investment. At the same time, appropriate safeguards should protect existing legitimate tenure rights to ensure, for instance, that land negotiations or transactions do not lead to the displacement, the loss of livelihoods, and more limited access to land for the local population. The legislation can provide for *ex ante* and *ex post* environmental and social impact assessments for land acquisitions exceeding a certain area to ensure that land allocation follows a transparent and inclusive process

Land tenure rights constitute a common cause for conflicts, for instance between investors and local communities due to disputes over land over which the latter had informal land use rights and due to the lack of transparency, especially on the conditions and process for land acquisition. Competent, efficient, transparent and independent institutions should be set up to resolve land disputes. Negotiation, mediation and arbitration can facilitate a fair and accessible justice.

Intellectual property rights protection

Intellectual property rights provide an incentive to invest in research and development, fostering the creation of innovative products and processes. They also give their holders the confidence to share new technologies through, *i.a.* joint ventures and licensing agreements. In this way, successful innovations are diffused within and across economies, bringing higher productivity and growth.

Intellectual property can have significant value, and hence good registration systems are crucial. Most importantly, the protection granted to intellectual property needs to strike a balance between the need to foster innovation and competitive markets and society's interests in having new products priced affordably.

The intellectual property rights regime is of concern not only to large firms and multinational enterprises but also to SMEs. A driving force behind innovation, SMEs often need to reinforce their potential to invest in innovation activities. They tend to underutilise the intellectual property system. Measures to make the system more accessible may thus help to attract investment in research and development and to transmit the positive spillovers to society that such investment embodies.

Foreign direct investment can be an important conduit for technology transfer among countries and the strength of the intellectual property regime will influence the willingness of foreign technology holders to invest. The empirical evidence suggests that where rights are strong, foreign companies are not only more likely to invest but are also more willing to share technologies with local partners and more likely to engage in local research and development.

Contract enforcement and dispute settlement

The ability to make and enforce contracts and resolve disputes is fundamental if markets are to function properly. Good enforcement procedures enhance predictability in commercial relationships by assuring investors that their contractual rights will be upheld promptly by local courts. When procedures for enforcing contracts are overly bureaucratic and cumbersome or when contract disputes cannot be resolved in a timely and cost effective manner, companies may restrict their activities. Traders may depend more heavily on personal and family connections; banks may reduce the amount of lending because of doubts about their ability to collect on debts or obtain control of property pledged as collateral to secure loans; and transactions may tend to be conducted on a cash-only basis. This limits the funding available for business expansion and slows down trade, investment, economic growth and development.

The court system has a fundamental role in enforcing contracts and in settling disputes, both among private actors and between an investor and the state. It provides key public goods in making interpretations of the law available to the public. The efficiency, effectiveness, integrity and independence of courts are important considerations for all investors, including foreign enterprises and SMEs. The court system can be made more attractive to investors by strengthening the independence of judges, efficient and predictable court procedures and the effective execution of judgments. Many governments have created specialised commercial courts to handle business disputes.

Alternative dispute resolution mechanisms, including arbitration, mediation and conciliation, are also available and increasingly used for resolving commercial disputes. Where such proceedings are confidential, however, they do not contribute to the development of the law, unlike with court cases. When disputes are resolved through arbitration outside of the country, national laws should ensure that domestic courts recognise and enforce these decisions in accordance with applicable international standards.

International investment agreements

The general purpose of international investment agreements is the promotion and protection of investments from one contracting party in the territory of the other contracting party. They provide, with variations in scope and content, for standards of treatment of investors and their investments, including:

- national treatment;
- guarantees against expropriation without compensation;
- guarantees of fair and equitable treatment or the international minimum standard of treatment;
- full protection and security;
- investor-state dispute settlement, allowing covered foreign investors to bring arbitration claims against host governments where they consider that treaty guarantees have been breached.

Approaches to investment treaty-making vary across countries and over time, as well as between the most common bilateral investment treaties and free trade agreements with an investment chapter. The *Framework* does not discuss whether or not governments should sign investment agreements or what an agreement should look like. Rather, it asks questions to help governments consider some of the key policy issues raised by such agreements and what measures could accompany the decision to offer specific protections to international investors. When deciding to conclude international investment agreements, governments should first and foremost ensure that they have the capacity to implement commitments and the ability to negotiate agreements that ensure sustainable development objectives.

Investment agreements provide an additional layer of security to covered foreign investors and can offer recourse to international investment arbitration to resolve investor-state disputes. Investors need some assurance that any dispute with the government will be dealt with fairly and swiftly, particularly in countries where investors have concerns about the reliability and independence of domestic courts. Such agreements may also help countries to improve their own domestic legislation covering investment. These considerations have led to the negotiation and signature of over 3 000 bilateral investment treaties, particularly in the 1990s.

The proliferation of bilateral and regional investment treaties and the multiplication of arbitral awards have contributed to an increasingly complex international investment policy landscape. Fewer bilateral treaties are being signed and more efforts are being concentrated on regional trade agreements with an investment chapter. There is a trend in both developed and developing countries towards refining and modernising the structure and content of investment treaties including increasing clarity of core provisions such as, *inter alia*, the definition of investment, fair and equitable treatment, and the rules for settling investor-state disputes.

Government exposure to international investment arbitration has been receiving increasing attention. The number of claims remains modest in comparison with the huge amounts of international investment that is covered by such provisions, but arbitration can nevertheless be costly for states that face claims, not only in terms of legal fees but also of the possible claims which can amount to hundreds of millions or even billions of dollars. An OECD-hosted Freedom of Investment Roundtable has analysed and discussed extensively investor-state dispute settlement mechanisms, including by developing a database of provisions in a broad range of investment treaties.

Whatever approach a government adopts towards international investment agreements, complementary measures can help to ensure that treaties are consistent with domestic priorities and reduce the risk of disputes leading to international arbitration. All relevant ministries should be involved in the negotiation process to ensure that all parts of government are aware of any commitments and to help point out any potential inconsistencies between those commitments and domestic legislation. As in all policy areas, governments should consult widely with all stakeholders, including foreign investors, and consider institutional dispute avoidance mechanisms, such as by offering ombudsman services to investors to try to resolve problems before they lead to disputes.

Notwithstanding the potential benefits of having signed international investment agreements, they should not be used by governments as a substitute for long-term improvements in the domestic business environment. Any active approach to international treaty making should be accompanied by measures to improve the capacity, efficiency and independence of the domestic court system, the quality of a country's legal framework, and the strength of national institutions responsible for implementing and enforcing such legislation.

Core questions and principles

Overall legal framework for investment

1. Has the government established a clear and comprehensive legal and regulatory framework for the conduct of business and investment activities?
2. How does the government ensure that the laws and regulations dealing with investment, their implementation and enforcement are consistent, clear, transparent, readily accessible and do not impose undue burdens?
3. How does the government balance policy flexibility needs against efforts to increase legal stability and predictability and the objective of maximising the contribution of investment to development?
4. Does the development of laws, treaties and regulations involve stakeholder consultations and are all relevant ministries and other public bodies involved?

Non-discrimination and national treatment

5. Consistent with its overall development strategy, has the government established non-discrimination as a general principle underpinning laws and regulations governing investment?
6. Is the economic impact of remaining restrictions, including on attracting investment, periodically reviewed to assess their costs against their intended public purpose?
7. Have the authorities explored other non-discriminatory means to secure their policy objectives?
8. Are restrictions (e.g. screening, foreign equity restrictions, key personnel, profit repatriation) easily identifiable for investors and formulated in a transparent manner?

Land tenure

9. Is land legislation clear and easily accessible to land users and is land management efficient and transparent? How are land rights allocated, administered and protected at national and sub-national levels?
10. What steps have been taken to improve land tenure security for domestic and foreign, large and small land users?

Intellectual property rights

11. Has the government ratified relevant international conventions and implemented laws and regulations to protect intellectual property rights?
12. How is the goal of fostering innovation and investment in R&D balanced against the public interest in terms of access to goods and services and knowledge?
13. Does the IP regime provide sufficient protection to encourage and secure technology transfers from foreign to domestic firms?
14. What strategies, policies and programmes have been developed to meet the intellectual property needs of SMEs?

Contract enforcement, domestic dispute settlement and commercial arbitration

15. Is the system of dispute settlement effective and widely accessible to all investors, including SMEs and foreign investors?
16. What alternative systems of dispute settlement are available to manage commercial and investment disputes?
17. Has the government ratified and implemented international commercial arbitration conventions? Are foreign commercial arbitration awards enforced in the courts in accordance with international standards?

Expropriation regime

18. What explicit and well-defined limits on the ability to expropriate has the government established in law and in practice?
19. What constitutional or legal safeguards guarantee that expropriation measures are taken only in a non-discriminatory manner, for a public purpose, under due process of law, and against fair compensation?
20. What judicial and administrative appeal mechanisms exist for reviewing or contesting decisions on the expropriation and on the amount of compensation?
21. How does the legal protection against expropriation provided in domestic laws compare with that accorded in investment treaties?

Investment treaty policy

22. What is the government's policy toward international investment agreements? What is the policy towards investor state dispute settlement?
23. Has the government ratified and implemented the ICSID Convention?
24. How does the government balance its sovereign right to regulate against the importance of providing legal certainty for investors?
25. Does the government attempt to assess the impact of its approach to IIAs on inward investment and on overall economic development?

Supplemental questions

Overall legal framework for investment

Legal framework	• What laws and regulations are in place to protect and regulate/ govern investment and business activities? • Is there a stand-alone investment law? If so, does it cover both foreign and domestic investment under the same umbrella? Does it provide for protection provisions? What regulations of investment does it set out?
Transparency and predictability	• Are there well established consultation mechanisms to enable investors and other interested stakeholders to participate in designing and monitoring investment laws and regulations? • How are legal amendments and draft bills made available to the public? • How are foreign and other investors informed about the formalities for registering a company? • What steps have been taken to ensure and monitor consistency among various regulations and legislations that constitute the investment regulatory framework? • Which institutions are involved in investment policy design and implementation? What are their respective roles?

Non-discrimination and national treatment

Establishing equivalent treatment	• Does domestic law generally provide for non-discrimination against foreign investors? If so, what is its scope and application (e.g. sub-national authorities apply national treatment)? • How much discretion do officials have in applying restrictions to foreign investment and are there safeguards in place to avoid non-arbitrary use of this discretion? • How does the government strike a balance between offering national treatment and preserving national interests, including the promotion of local enterprise development?
The nature of exceptions to national treatment	Do any of the following restrictions apply to foreign investment: • screening procedures for FDI entry, whether across-the-board or sector-based? • more extensive licensing requirements for foreign investors than for domestic investors? • foreign equity ownership ceilings in different sectors? • limits on access for foreign established enterprises to local finance and incentives (e.g. tax concessions)? • restrictions on access to land for foreign investors? • restrictions on legal establishment (e.g. subsidiaries or branches)? • limits on access to specific markets (e.g. public procurement, privatisations)? • performance requirements (e.g. local content rules)? • other discriminatory practices (e.g. nationality based restrictions on boards, limits on key personnel)?
Screening of foreign investment	If the government screens foreign investment (these questions do not apply to screening based solely on national security), • What are the criteria for approval? Are they clear and can the time and cost involved be estimated? • If national interest forms part of the criteria, how is it defined? • If a net economic benefit test is applied, is the burden of proof on the investor or the government? • How much discretion does the authority have? Are measures in place to prevent and detect bribery for the purpose of influencing such discretion? • Do decisions have to be rendered within a specified time? • Are the criteria within the competence of the agency to assess? • Are the reasons for rejecting a project published? • Can the investor appeal the decision before an independent administrative or judicial body? • Are investor commitments monitored once the project is approved? If so, what is the sanctioning procedure when commitments are not met? • Are screening policies subject to periodic review of their effectiveness and necessity? • How does the government minimise the administrative burden for investors undergoing screening? • How many projects are rejected or modified each year on average? • Do pending screening processes suspend the investment?
Transparency and periodic review of discriminatory restrictions on foreign investment	• Is there a publicly available negative list of sectors and activities where foreign investors face restrictions? If so, is it section to periodic review and is there a mechanism to reduce restrictions over time? • Is the negative list complete and with a sufficient degree of sectoral detail, including underlying laws and regulations? • What policy objectives are addressed by discriminating on the basis of ownership of project equity? • Does the government consider whether alternative policy instruments, such as support for SME development (see section on *Investment Promotion and Facilitation*), could achieve the same goals more effectively? • Does the country benchmark the scope of discriminatory restrictions in its laws and in practice with other similar economies? • How does the country compare with peers in the region or at a similar level of economic development in terms of its discriminatory measures? • Does it periodically review the list of restrictions based on an analysis of their costs and benefits or on a narrower regulatory impact analysis? • Does the government canvass the views of foreign and domestic investors and other relevant stakeholders on the relevance of restrictions?
Free transfer of funds	• Do restrictions on the transfers of investment-related capital and profits exist? If so, how do they operate? • To which types of transfer do they apply (e.g. profits, dividends, interest and royalty receipts, original capital, capital appreciation, proceeds from liquidation, payments received as compensation for property expropriation, settlement of disputes etc., and earnings of personnel engaged from abroad in connection with an investment)? • Do they apply to domestic as well as foreign investors? • Do the rules apply to both new and existing investments? • Are there formal notification procedures for capital transfers? • Do the rules apply both to inward and outward investment? • Under which conditions may new restrictions be imposed (e.g. a balance of payments crisis)? • Has the government reviewed these restrictions and their effect on attracting international investment? • Have investors complained of high costs (e.g. because of excessive exchange transaction charges) or unreasonable delays (e.g. because of numerous and complex verification procedures)? • What is the scope for arbitrary and discretionary decisions regarding the transfer of investment-related capital (e.g. on the choice of exchange rate values)?

Land ownership and registration

Land tenure security	• Are rules in place clarifying the scale, scope and nature of allowable transactions in tenure rights? How are transfers exceeding a certain scale approved? Are land tenure rights limited in time? • Are there any restrictions/conditions to land use by land category (such as cultivating certain crops on agricultural land)? What measures are taken if land rights holders do not comply with such conditions? • Do foreign individuals or corporations face specific restrictions to obtain land tenure rights? Do they have to comply with specific administrative procedures? • What measures have been taken to protect legitimate land tenure rights, including public, private, communal, collective, indigenous and customary rights?
Land registration	• What are the challenges faced by the land administration to register the remaining land area? What procedures are required at national and sub-national levels to register land? • What agencies are responsible for developing land use plans and for registering land? Do they have clear and well-defined responsibilities to ensure smooth land use planning and registration? • What proportion of land has been mapped or formally registered (by land category)? How long does it take and how much does it cost to register land? • How reliable and accurate is the land registry? Is it easily accessible? • How long does it take and how much does it cost to change land from one category to another? • What measures have been taken to ensure that all land users, including vulnerable groups, can register land?
Land market	• What efforts have been made to support the development of a well-functioning land market while ensuring a fair and equitable access to land? • Have some recent efforts been undertaken to promote transparent land management? • Are there restrictions to selling, transferring, leasing, bequeathing or mortgaging land tenure rights or using them as collateral? How long does it take and how much does it cost to sell, transfer, bequeath or mortgage land tenure rights? • Have land use plans been developed countrywide? What stakeholders are involved in negotiating them? • Can land users easily access land use plans?
Land disputes	• What agencies are responsible for resolving land disputes? Do they have clear and well-defined responsibilities to ensure prompt land dispute resolution? • Do they face any challenges in providing an equitable, affordable and efficient system for resolving land disputes? How long does it take and how much does it cost to resolve land disputes? • What are the most common causes of land conflicts?
Responsible business conduct	• What measures are in place to ensure transparency and information disclosure related to land-based investments, including transparency of lease/concession contract terms? • What mechanisms are in place to conduct meaningful, effective and good-faith consultations with land rights holders, in particular indigenous peoples or local communities? • What measures are in place to minimise the physical and/or economic displacement of legitimate tenure right holders? Under what circumstances can the government expropriate land tenure rights holders? • What measures are in place to ensure prompt, adequate and fair compensation of land tenure rights holders in case of expropriation? How is the value of compensation, including the land value, determined? • What measures are in place to minimise adverse environmental impacts and promote sustainable land use?

Intellectual property rights

Legal framework	• What laws and regulations are in place to protect ownership rights to intellectual assets? • How much protection and coverage do these laws provide? Do regulations and laws contain provisions that protect IP beyond the minimum requirements of the TRIPS agreement? • How does the country ensure that provisions of the WTO TRIPS agreements are properly enforced? • Is the country a party to international treaties and conventions on intellectual property, including patents and copyrights? If not, what deters the country from doing so?
Efficient registration	• How efficient is the registration process in terms of costs involved and time required? Is it reliable and secure? • What are the procedures for handling intellectual property registered in other jurisdictions? • How does the IP office facilitate procedural and administrative issues relating to the application process (e.g. availability of regional services, help desks within IP offices, information kits, web sites and online registration procedures)? • How much do businesses use the system and what is their filing success rate? Is usage restricted to large firms? Do universities and public research institutes seek intellectual property protection when engaging in innovation? • What are the costs of filing and obtaining IP (e.g. application, publication and maintenance fees, translation costs when applying for protection in other markets), as well as those incurred to maintain and enforce IP rights? • How long does it take to register IP rights? • Is there a strategy in place to help meet the specific needs of SMEs? Are there discount rates in place to support the registration and enforcement of IP rights by SMEs?

Awareness raising	Does the IP office or responsible agency: • organise information seminars and campaigns on IP and provide capacity building on how to file for IP protection? • produce practical IP guides and other materials targeted to specific customer groups? • collect and disseminate case studies illustrating good practices in applying for and enforcing IP protection? • What programmes are in place to improve access to existing knowledge, especially among SMEs?
Enforcement and dispute settlement mechanisms	• What mechanisms are in place to enforce a country's IP system and to resolve disputes? Do they limit the cost to business of enforcing and monitoring the use of their IP rights make the IP system more accessible? • What are the criminal and civil penalties for transgressing IP laws? • Does the country feature on watch-lists based on external perceptions of the extent of enforcement of IP rights (e.g. USTR Special 301 reports)? • Is the judicial system efficient to address IP disputes? Are there specialised courts to hear IP-related cases, with judges trained in IP law? • Are there procedures for settling IP disputes out of court? • To what extent is mediation available to settle IP-related cases? • Has the government created specific institutions for settling IP disputes? If so, how efficient are they and how many cases per year do they deal with? Are they commonly used by SMEs and other small entities? • Is there a market for IP insurance to help reduce the costs of litigation? If not, are there plans to develop one? • Does each agency involved have well-defined responsibilities?
A balanced innovation policy framework	• How do IP laws and regulations fit within the country's overall innovation strategy? Are IP institutions only in charge of the enforcement of IP protection, or do they also have a role in promoting innovation policies? • Does the government promote close ties and collaboration between universities and businesses to commercialise inventions and new technologies, e.g. by laws that enable universities to share royalties from jointly-produced innovations (see also the section on *Investment Promotion and Facilitation* and on *Developing Human Resources for Investment*)? • Are there special provisions defining circumstances when the state can use patents outside of normal patent protection rules on the grounds of the wider public interest? • How does the government assess the effectiveness of its innovation framework in developing domestic R&D capacity and new technology? • To what extent is the existing framework conducive to promoting technology transfer among firms (see also section on *Investment Promotion and Facilitation*)?

Contract enforcement and investment dispute settlement

Effective contract enforcement	• Is the jurisdiction for hearing contractual disputes clearly defined in law (e.g. for contracts involving foreign entities, government and state-owned enterprises) and in which courts (e.g. local, specialised, small-claim courts, administrative courts)? • Are any limits on jurisdictional and enforcement powers (e.g. prohibition on seizing state property to satisfy court judgments) transparent? • Do national laws define the conditions of validity and enforcement of foreign judgments and foreign arbitral awards? Please provide reference to the laws.
Institutional requirements to support contract enforcement	• Are there specialised commercial courts? If not, do judges have any special training to hear complex commercial disputes? • Are there independent surveys of the integrity and independence of the judiciary? • What is the degree of efficiency of the court system (e.g. case load of judges, backlog of cases, level of funding and capacity of judges)? • What are the case management practices of the court system (e.g. use of information technology for filing and tracking cases, for implementing procedural and jurisdictional rules, and for recording and disseminating reasoned case histories)? • Do courts enforce contractual agreements and settlements?
The cost of enforcing contracts	• What are the estimated costs of enforcing contracts, including e.g. court fees and taxes? • Are there small claims courts? If so, are they accessible to SMEs? Are they available at local level? • What is the average length of time required to enforce a contract through the court system? • What are the costs of pre-trial and trial procedures mandated by law (e.g. evidentiary standards, cooling-off periods) or court regulation (e.g. time limits for court actions and on the parties to present evidence) and procedural rules between the parties needed to file a case, during the trial and judgment period and to enforce the judgment? • Do procedural rules depend on the nature of the dispute and the court that is hearing the dispute (e.g. small-claim courts)?

Alternative dispute settlement mechanisms	• Do national laws recognise alternative dispute resolution mechanisms (e.g. foreign-based conciliation commissions and arbitral tribunals) and honour and enforce their decisions? • Are alternative dispute resolution mechanisms (e.g. arbitration, mediation, conciliation) for hearing and settling investment disputes encouraged? • Do investors have the right to choose an alternative dispute settlement method (e.g. international commercial or investment arbitration)? • What are the relative costs and efficacy of the alternatives available and the methods of involvement by the official sector to enforce settlement agreements? • How do rules on the procedures for commercial disputes prevent or limit practices of "forum shopping" and of dilatory measures?
Commercial arbitration	• Do practices or restrictions on agreements to arbitrate disputes affect the use and effectiveness of arbitration (e.g. mandatory procedures for the conduct of arbitration proceedings, regulations that limit who can serve as an arbitrator)? • Can national courts interfere with pending arbitration proceedings (e.g. accepting to hear a dispute that the parties had agreed to submit to international arbitration)? • How clear is supporting national legislation?

Expropriation regime

Defining the power to expropriate property	• Do laws that permit property confiscation expressly limit the conditions under which the government may expropriate private property for public purposes? • Do legal standards exist for determining when an expropriation event has occurred? • Does the law permitting expropriation discriminate, such as on the basis of nationality? • Does such a law establish the right to adequate compensation? • Does such a law allow for an appeals process? • Do procedures exist for calculating compensation (e.g. specifying the factors and methods that can be used, such as purchase price, resale value, depreciation, goodwill etc.)? • While it is not feasible to list every circumstance in which the state may take private property in the public interest, have the authorities made efforts to define the concept and to place boundaries on the scope of the public interest? • Does expropriation of land or other property by the government have to be for public purposes? • Does the government consider means other than expropriation, such as, for example, by giving government the right of first refusal on land transactions?
Compensation for expropriation	• How is the amount of compensation calculated? • Which factors are taken into consideration (e.g. the value of intangible assets, depreciation, damage to property)? • What legal standards are applied and what practices are adopted (e.g. use of third-party expert valuations, payment of interest)? • In cases where there is no readily available market price, how does the government avoid arbitrary procedures? • What is the median time taken to effect compensation following an expropriation event? • Does the government benchmark itself against peers in terms of the speed with which investors are compensated? • How is compensation paid? Are payments fully realisable (e.g. paid in cash) and freely transferable (e.g. convertible into another currency, or payable in a hard currency)? • When non-pecuniary settlements are offered (e.g. resettling displaced persons), does the government consult with those directly concerned? Are such persons resettled near to the previous location? Does the new location offer a similar amenity value and a comparable quality? • Are case histories of expropriation events brought to commissions or arbitral tribunals and consultations with stakeholders analysed to gain insights and feedback from the process? • Are there a disproportionate number of cases in a specific sector or involving foreign enterprises? • How does the government ensure adequate compensation for land acquisitions and resettlement as part of large-scale investment projects (e.g. mining, hydropower, agriculture and plantations)?
Regulatory actions tantamount to expropriation	• Does domestic law recognise the concept of indirect expropriation or regulatory takings? Are the rules reasonably clear? Does the government provide guidance to government agencies on how to distinguish practices that may constitute indirect expropriation? • Does the government collect, synthesise and communicate the reasons from relevant cases? • For events that were determined to be cases of indirect expropriation, was the property owner compensated? What was the measure of compensation?

Independent channels to review or contest expropriation decisions	• Are there administrative and judicial review processes available to review expropriation decisions? • Does a court or tribunal, whether domestic or supranational, have the authority to review decisions regarding expropriation of property and to give effect to its decisions? • What restrictions, if any, exist on who has the right to contest an expropriation event? • What are the modalities for filing an appeal or contesting an expropriation decision? • What is the technical capacity of the court or tribunal to hear contested expropriation cases? • Is the appeals body independent from the agency ordering the expropriation? Does it have the power to review and if necessary overturn government agency decisions regarding expropriation and compensation to owners of expropriated property? • Are the grounds on which a decision can be contested clear and transparent (*e.g.* documented procedural rules)?

Investment treaty policy

Investment treaty policy	• Have bilateral investment treaties (BITs) or Free Trade Agreements with an investment chapter been signed? Are they in force? With which countries or regions? Are major investor countries covered? • Do IIAs support the liberalisation of investment flows or only the protection of established investors? Does ISDS apply to liberalisation commitments? Has the government's approach to treaty policy evolved? Are there important variations between IIAs? Has the government developed a model BIT and, if so, how has this evolved over time? What has been the experience in using the model in negotiations? • What standards of treatment does the government provide through its IIAs? Has the government integrated sustainable development and other public welfare considerations into its treaties (e.g. provisions on RBC, labour rights, environmental and public health policies)? • Some of the topics covered in other questions in this section and in other sections (e.g. trade-related investment measures in the section on *Trade Policy*) relate to provisions of international investment agreements.
Expropriation and national treatment	• Do the IIAs contain a provision on expropriation? • Do they contain a provision on indirect expropriation? Is the scope of protection for indirect expropriation clear (eg. through a clarification of its meaning)? • Is national treatment embodied in international investment agreements that the country is party to and, if so, at what stage (i.e. pre- or post-establishment) does it apply? Do these agreements grant most-favoured-nation treatment to investors and investments? If so, at what phase (i.e. pre- or post-establishment)? • Is national treatment dependent on a reciprocal commitment or deferred to a later date? • Are general exceptions to the principle of national treatment contained in IIAs (*e.g.* to maintain public health or to protect national security)? • Are there subject-specific exceptions (e.g. intellectual property, taxation conventions)? • Are there sector-specific exceptions (e.g. specific industries, such as financial services and transport)? • Are exceptions based on an explicit, clearly defined and detailed rationale? • In international agreements signed by the country, does national treatment apply only to areas and industries identified in a 'positive' list (e.g. GATS agreements)?
Other investor protection clauses	• Do IIAs define the type of covered investments? Do they explicitly exclude certain forms of investment? • How do IIAs address investment liberalisation? • Do IIAs contain most-favoured-nation (MFN) treatment clauses? Is their scope of application clear (eg. with regard to whether they are limited to domestic measures or extend to other investment treaties; or, if they apply to other treaties, whether they are limited to substantive provisions or extend to procedural provisions)? • Has the government considered the potential impact of MFN clauses on efforts to reform treaty practices? • Do treaties contain clauses on fair and equitable treatment or on the international minimum standard of treatment? How much discretion is left to arbitrators in applying the clauses? Are relevant government actors aware of the potential scope of the clauses (eg., for some versions, in potentially applying to non-contractual "commitments" made by government officials)? • Are claims by shareholders for reflective loss permitted under IIAs? (Shareholders' reflective loss is incurred as a result of injury to "their" company, typically a loss in value of the shares; it is generally contrasted with direct injury to shareholder rights, such as interference with shareholder voting rights.) Under what conditions? • Do IIAs contain umbrella clauses? Is their scope of application well-defined? Is it understood by relevant government actors? Are there important variations, between IIAs signed by the country, in the degree of protection granted to foreign investors?
Investor-state dispute settlement clause	• Do IIAs provide for ISDS? To what degree do IIAs regulate ISDS and how does the degree of regulation compare with treaty practice in other countries including as analysed by the FOI Roundtable? • Has the government faced claims under IIAs? What treaty provisions were at issue? What were the outcomes? How does the government view the claims process and how has the government reacted to the claims?

International arbitration instruments	• Has the government ratified the 1966 Convention on the Settlement of Investment Disputes between States and Nationals of Other States (ICSID or Washington Convention) and the 1958 New York Convention on Recognition and Enforcement of Arbitral Awards? • If the country is not a party to ICSID, is the ICSID Additional Facility used? • Has the government introduced national legislation and procedural rules so that foreign arbitral awards are recognised and enforced by local courts without undue delay? • Does the government participate in intergovernmental forums that facilitate arbitration and other forms of dispute settlement involving states (e.g. the Permanent Court of Arbitration)?
Transparency	• How do IIAs address the issue of transparency of ISDS? • Are cases transparent in practice (party submissions, arbitral decisions and awards, etc.)? • Has the government committed to apply the UNCITRAL Rules on transparency to already existing investment treaties? • Where transparency depends on the agreement of the disputing parties, is agreement to publish awards frequently obtained? • Is information about cases involving the country communicated widely (e.g. posted on relevant government websites)?
Building capacity	• Who has authority and responsibility for initiating negotiations? • Is there a dedicated unit responsible for evaluating the experience with existing agreements? Does it inform the government's position vis-à-vis new agreements? • How does the government strengthen the capacity within its public service for treaty negotiation? • Does the government have sufficient expertise and capacity to respond effectively to treaty claims by investors? • Has the government made efforts to identify and train individuals who could be suitable investment law arbitrators? Has it made suitable nominations of arbitrators to standing panels (eg. at ICSID)?
Effective compliance with IIAs	• How does the government ensure consistency between the commitments in IIAs and domestic legislation? • What efforts are made to communicate to government agencies the implications of IIAs for their areas of responsibility (e.g. implementation guides)?

Additional resources

Websites

OECD Investment, *www.oecd.org/investment/*.

OECD

Gaukrodger, D. (2013), "Investment Treaties as Corporate Law: Shareholder Claims and Issues of Consistency", *OECD Working Papers on International Investment*, No. 2013/03, OECD Publishing, Paris, *http://dx.doi.org/10.1787/5k3w9t44mt0v-en.*

Gaukrodger, D. and K. Gordon (2012), "Investor-State Dispute Settlement: A Scoping Paper for the Investment Policy Community", *OECD Working Papers on International Investment*, No. 2012/03, OECD Publishing, Paris, *http://dx.doi.org/10.1787/5k46b1r85j6f-en.*

Gordon, K. and J. Pohl (2011), "Environmental Concerns in International Investment Agreements: A Survey", *OECD Working Papers on International Investment*, No. 2011/01, OECD Publishing, Paris, *http://dx.doi.org/10.1787/5kg9mq7scrjh-en.*

Gordon, K., J. Pohl and M. Bouchard (2014), "Investment Treaty Law, Sustainable Development and Responsible Business Conduct: A Fact Finding Survey", *OECD Working Papers on International Investment*, No. 2014/01, OECD Publishing, Paris, *http://dx.doi.org/10.1787/5jz0 xvgx1zlt-en.*

OECD (2014), *Policy Framework for Investment in Agriculture*, OECD Publishing, Paris, *http:// dx.doi.org/ 10.1787/9789264212725-en.*

OECD (2015), OECD FDI Regulatory Restrictiveness Index, *www.oecd.org/investment/fdiindex.htm.*

Pohl, J., K. Mashigo and A. Nohen (2012), "Dispute Settlement Provisions in International Investment Agreements: A Large Sample Survey", *OECD Working Papers on International Investment*, No. 2012/02, OECD Publishing, Paris, *http://dx.doi.org/10.1787/5k8xb71nf628-en.*

UNCTAD

UNCTAD (2012), *Investment Policy Framework for Sustainable Development*, United Nations Conference for Trade and Development, Geneva.

APEC

APEC (2011), *APEC Non-Binding Investment Principles*, Asia-Pacific Economic Co-operation, Investment Experts' Group.

Other

CFS (2014), *Principles for Responsible Investment in Agriculture and Food Systems*, Committee on World Food Security (CFS).

FAO (2012), *Voluntary Guidelines on the Responsible Governance of Tenure of Land, Fisheries and Forests*, Food and Agriculture Organisation of the United Nations.

ICC (2012), *ICC Guidelines for International Investment*, International Chamber of Commerce, Paris.

Policy Framework for Investment
2015 Edition

2. Investment promotion and facilitation

Investment promotion and facilitation can be powerful means to attract investment and maximise its contribution to development, but their success depends on the quality of investment-related policies and on the overall investment climate. Successful promotion requires a careful calculation of how to employ resources most effectively guided by evaluations of costs and benefits; badly designed investment promotion and facilitation strategies can be costly and ineffective. Also, investment promotion and facilitation depends by and large on the quality of investment-related policies.

This section aims to provide key principles for effective investment promotion and facilitation, including co-ordinating and evaluating investment promotion activities, while providing options to strengthen the development impact of investment through local enterprise development. It provides avenues for achieving the twin objectives of attracting responsible investment and fostering local development.

Promoting and facilitating investment are two very different types of activities. One is about promoting a country or a region as an investment destination, while the other is about making it easy for investors to establish or expand their existing investments. Effective investment promotion leverages the strong points of a country's investment environment, highlights profitable investment opportunities and helps to identify local partners. In terms of facilitation, effective one-stop-shops with single-point authority can be a critical factor in investment decisions, especially if they cut down the investor's transaction costs: complex administrative burdens represent significant barriers to investment. Effective investment facilitation can also reduce corruption risks by decreasing the number of steps involved in the decision-making process. A core mandate of investment facilitation includes filling an information gap created by incoherent or inaccurate policies. Investment facilitation can thus provide investors with much needed clarity vis-à-vis public administration and policies.

Governments can adopt a wide array of investment promotion and facilitation structures. If an investment promotion agency (IPA) is to be established, it can be created as part of a ministry or as an independent agency. It should have a clear mandate and its staff should have private sector experience. Its structure should be lean and efficient, and its board should consist of both public and private sector representatives. Yet, many functions of an IPA can be undertaken within existing structures without creating costly additional agencies. Most IPAs concentrate on attracting greenfield investment, but promoting re-investments and business expansions can be important, particularly in promoting investments in higher valued-added activities. Mergers and acquisitions are not proactively targeted but information services are often provided to facilitate these transactions where and when warranted.

One size does not fit all, and different approaches are suitable for different countries and different target enterprises (e.g. big and small firms, those in the formal and informal economies, in different sectors, those run by women and minority groups, etc.). Some countries have contracted out investment prospecting, with mixed results. For those with small budgets, the focus should be on investment facilitation, reducing the burden on investors. While many IPAs use fiscal incentives as an investment promotion tool, the *Policy Framework for Investment* addresses these in the *Tax Policy* section, given their impact on governments' efforts in mobilising domestic resources.

In terms of investment promotion instruments, experience has shown that targeted promotion missions abroad in carefully identified growth markets and sectors are more effective than expensive international marketing campaigns. Such missions should be carefully managed and co-ordinated with sub-national IPAs to avoid duplication. Countries should also make use of their international representations, such as the diplomatic corps. Establishing a system for handling investor inquiries can help ensure that potential and existing investors receive adequate customer care. Some IPAs have even established key accounts for specific investments to be able to address policy and operational bottlenecks more efficiently. A well-designed and regularly updated website has also become a necessary tool for IPAs, providing a platform to showcase the economy and investment opportunities.

After-care services for investors are vital, especially in retaining investors, just as after-sales functions within a private company aim to sustain customer loyalty. At the same time, after-care adds value to a service or product beyond the selling point – the decision to invest or reinvest. Many countries have struggled to retain investors after an investment peak. Attracting new investors is more challenging and costly compared to supporting reinvestment and expansion, which account for a significant share of all investments. Good after-care and policy advocacy, including transmitting investors' feedback for more effective policy making, can be the determining factor in a decision to reinvest and help address investment climate challenges. The most effective IPAs devote substantial resources to policy advocacy and to resolving investors' complaints.

Successful countries in attracting investment have mastered a whole-of-government approach to investment promotion and facilitation. Effective co-ordination among various authorities with investment promotion mandates, including at local government levels, and implementing agencies (be they in charge of investment promotion, export and trade promotion, special economic zones, business registration, or land allocation) is a daunting task. Many economies have pushed through reforms to decentralise investment promotion and facilitation. Delegating some functions of IPAs to the sub-national level may contribute to swifter management of investment applications. These experiences have been mixed, with significant challenges remaining in the co-ordination of the different agencies, addressing the often weaker capacities at the provincial level, while aiming to ensure consistency with the national and sub-national development plans.

Investment promotion can encourage countries' participation in the global economy. The attraction of export-oriented foreign direct investment (FDI) has enabled countries to shift quickly towards a manufacturing-based economy in which economic growth is driven by rapidly expanding exports. The record from this export performance speaks for itself, but so too does the manifest failure in many cases to translate this export success based on FDI into broader and more durable impacts on host economies. Not only have exports been limited to a small number of products (usually intermediate ones) and sectors, but to varying degrees these export sectors have been virtual foreign enclaves within host countries. The latter have often been characterised by low value-addition, low wages, and a poor record of technology transfer. This highlights the importance of embedding investment promotion activities within a broader economic development strategy that involves investments in people and skills, improving connectivity of firms and markets, and building an open business environment to help countries benefit from global value chains (GVCs), while promoting responsible investment (see section on *Policies for Enabling Responsible Business Conduct*. In this regard, opportunities also exist for regional and sub-regional investment promotion and facilitation, as multinational enterprises (MNEs) often organise their supply chains across different economies.

Anchoring investors through deep linkages with the local economy is an effective investment retention strategy and can usefully complement after-care measures. Investor targeting and after-care services can attract investors and help keep them satisfied, but it is the broader and more sophisticated, and hence more complex, efforts to strengthen the investment ecosystem that will determine a country or region's competitiveness. This includes providing investors with competitive local suppliers, facilitating linkages with local firms, developing the necessary hard and soft infrastructure, including institutional support, and keeping policy and macro-economic fundamentals in order.

Business linkages between MNEs and domestic companies, especially smaller suppliers, contribute significantly to local development. Linkages can be effective avenues for the transfer of technology, knowledge and managerial and technical skills, depending on the appropriate policy setting and absorptive capacity of domestic suppliers. The importance of an enabling environment that is conducive to the growth and competitiveness of small and medium-sized enterprises (SMEs) in this regard is critical. This may involve SME promotion and support measures ranging from streamlining business regulations to targeted vocational training and business development services (see section on *Developing Human Resources for Investment*), as well as providing SMEs with know-how on establishing effective measures for responsible business conduct. These should accompany the crucial efforts to promote SME financing.

MNEs do not necessarily engage in linkages with domestic suppliers automatically. Many MNEs are bound by international contracting arrangements that tie them to international suppliers, offsetting the effectiveness of public policies to promote linkages. Investors with a tradition of working with and supporting local suppliers in their efforts to upgrade should thus be targeted.

Committed long-term relationships between MNEs and SMEs usually involve a transfer of technology and proprietary knowledge. Unless MNEs are given safeguards against intellectual "piracy" and illicit diffusion of their know-how, they will be reluctant to share technology, making intellectual property protection an important part of policies aimed at fostering business linkages (see section on *Investment Policy*). At the same time, market-seeking investors are often more prone to develop linkages, including forward linkages and associated spillovers, than are resource-seeking or export-oriented investors. FDI in upstream activities has at times been linked to higher productivity in local manufacturing and to an increase in local sourcing, thereby boosting a country's export competitiveness.

Many governments opt for special economic zones (SEZs) to attract investors, create jobs and increase export earnings. Common features include a geographically defined area, streamlined procedures – such as for customs, special regulations, tax holidays – which are often governed by a single administrative authority. A zone-based strategy may be effective in attracting investors in the short-run by offering adequate infrastructure, services and duty-free access for capital goods and other inputs. Yet, such zones have often stagnated in terms of sustaining innovation and competitiveness, failing in technological upgrading and new industry creation. Their overall contribution to national development is often questioned, particularly when labour or environmental standards within such zones are by law, or in practice, lower than in the general economy. Economic activities within free trade zones, allowing for import and export cost reduction measures, also tend to have weak linkages with the rest of the economy if not firmly embedded in a wider development agenda, including appropriate connectivity to the rest of the economy and reduced barriers to investment. Countries employing a zone-based strategy must be careful to ensure that the legal and regulatory framework for responsible business conduct, as well as measures to fight corruption, are applied to companies in the zone with the same level of diligence as elsewhere in the country.

Several economies have followed a more elaborate and comprehensive strategy of cluster development. The existence of industry clusters at the local level represents an important location factor for many MNEs. Dynamic clusters rely on the smooth interaction of a number of pillars, combining public policies and initiatives at the firm-level. Clusters typically exhibit the following characteristics, critical for their generation of new technology, innovation, and firm creation:

- Strong role of government (federal or state) in promoting stability and basic infrastructure;
- An institutional environment that stimulates technological acquisition and transfer, including the protection of intellectual property rights, well-designed science and technologies policies and the involvement of research and development institutions;
- Global connectivity of clusters through value chains and markets;
- Competent intermediary organisations to promote horizontal connectivity and co-ordination among actors and stakeholders.

A skilled workforce catering to the needs of investors is a vital part of the investment ecosystem. Creating an integrated framework to enhance skills is challenging, as it often needs to address the specifics of a higher-skilled export sector, a medium-skilled domestic economy, and a low-skill informal economy. The role of the private sector in developing skills is widespread in many economies, as businesses know best what skills they need. The section on *Developing Human Resources for Investment* looks at the various policy options for skills development in greater detail.

Core questions and principles

1. How does the government's investment promotion and facilitation strategy support the country's overall development goals and growth objectives?
2. How are investment promotion and facilitation measures developed, implemented, co-ordinated and evaluated?
3. What are the main measures and instruments to promote responsible and sustainable investment?
4. In its efforts to facilitate investment, how does the government streamline administrative procedures to ease of doing business and reduce the cost of investing?
5. To what extent does the government promote and maintain dialogue mechanisms with investors and policy advocacy to inform policy making?

6. How does the government promote business linkages, including those between foreign and domestic enterprises and in particular domestic SMEs?
7. How does the government's investment promotion strategy contribute to the integration into global and regional value chains?
8. Has the government used international and regional networks to promote investment?

Supplemental questions

Role of investment in development strategy	• Do investment and the benefits it can bring to the economy feature in national development plans and objectives? What is the specific expected role of FDI? • Does the government have a coherent inward investment promotion strategy in place that is in line with national economic development priorities? • How is the impact of private investment on the country's overall economic and development objectives addressed and assessed? • Is there a strategy for developing a sound, broad-based business environment and within this strategy, what role is given to investment promotion and facilitation? • What methodology is used to measure investment inflows into the country? • How does the government ensure it has good data on investment generation and expansion decisions to inform policy making?
Implementation of investment promotion and facilitation	• What agencies are mandated with promoting and facilitating investment? What is the institutional framework governing investment promotion and facilitation to ensure that activities are well co-ordinated? • To what extent have their structures, functions, missions, and legal status been informed by and benchmarked against international good practices? • How are the investment promotion agencies structured and who supervises them? • How are the various investment promotion and facilitation measures co-ordinated across agencies and different layers of the administration (national and subnational approaches, sectoral approaches)? • What measures are in place to ensure adequate capacity in various agencies to effectively undertake the functions pertaining to investment promotion and facilitation? • How are investment and trade promotion activities co-ordinated? • How are the investment promotion agencies funded? Do the investment promotion agencies generate their own financing through their services? • How does the government evaluate the efficiency and effectiveness of these agencies or programmes? • Is the government's performance in attracting investment benchmarked internationally?
Investment promotion	• What are the main objectives and core functions of the investment promotion agencies? • What instruments have been developed and used to promote investment? To what extent have these been informed by international good practices and internationally recognised standards? • How is coherence between investment promotion measures and other policy measures (e.g. trade policy, innovation and skills development, infrastructural development and labour, safety, environmental and anti-corruption policies) ensured? • Has the relative effectiveness of different strategies and instruments been evaluated? • Are specific sectors, markets and investors targeted as part of the investment promotion strategy? If so, on what basis? Do these include considerations of the potential investors' track record on responsible business conduct including environmental and social issues? • How does the government ensure flexibility in its targeting strategy to respond and adapt to new market demands and opportunities? • Has the government considered the impact of its targeting strategy on other sectors, including sub-sectors that can potentially support the sectors targeted? • Does the government make use of investment promotion missions abroad? • Is outward investment promoted and, if so, how is this promotion co-ordinated? • What mechanisms has the government established to evaluate the cost and benefits of investment incentives, their appropriate duration, and their transparency (See the *Tax Policy* section for a more detailed treatment of investment incentives)?
Investment facilitation	• How have administrative procedures been streamlined to reduce the cost of investing, simplify business registration procedures and reduce opportunities for corruption in related procedures? • How is effective communication with the private sector ensured to resolve issues related to establishing a business, obtaining licenses etc.? • In an effort to retain responsible investment and facilitate re-investment, does the government or its dedicated agencies provide adequate after-care services based on international good practices? • Has the government established one-stop-shops for investment? If yes, how is their efficiency monitored? Does the government use online technology and instruments to facilitate the implementation of business regulations and procedures? • How are investment facilitation measures benchmarked with competing countries? • Are promotion efforts concentrated in a few priority sectors or areas? If yes, based on what rationale?

Public-private sector dialogue	• What are the main public-private consultative platforms? What are the formal mechanisms and channels for government-investor dialogue? • Are investment promotion agencies involved in policy advocacy and are they consulted on matters having an impact on investment? • Does the government offer private sector ombudsman services? • How is the feedback from investors used in informing policy development, design and implementation?
Promoting business linkages	• How does the government promote linkages between businesses, especially between foreign affiliates and local enterprises? • Are match-making meetings and roundtables for investors and local firms that could act as suppliers (including SMEs) organised? Are databases of potential suppliers made available to foreign investors? What other activities and concrete measures does the government undertake to promote linkages? • What is the role of special economic zones (SEZs) in promoting investment and linkages? • Does the framework governing SEZs supports overall economic development objectives and avoid creating economic enclaves? Is the legal and regulatory framework for preventing and punishing business crimes, such as tax evasion, labour violations, environmental and safety violations, and corruption, applied to companies in SEZs with the same level of diligence as in the rest of the country? • Does the government support industry clusters? • How are ties between the government, the private sector and SME support institutions, including technical and vocational training institutions, developed to promote linkages? • What is the overall SME promotion strategy? What are the main public SME promotion initiatives and programmes? What are the main SME financing mechanisms and schemes (see section on *Financing Investment)*? • Has the government promoted business development services (BDS) to support domestic investors in addressing specific challenges (training, access to market information and finance, information on business opportunities)? • What private sector driven linkages initiatives exist (training by companies for their suppliers, support to financing of suppliers' activities, etc.)?
Integration in global value chains	• Is the investment promotion strategy aligned with the objectives of integrating in regional and global value chains (GVCs)? Do investment generation activities target the relevant type of investors or activities? • How are obstacles to better integration of local firms into regional and global value chains identified? • Do foreign investors and large domestic enterprises help to develop local firms, including SMEs, so as to strengthen the local supply base and increase local value addition? • How is the demand for skills from the private sector, including foreign investors, channelled to tertiary, vocational and technical training systems to avoid skills shortages and mismatches? What measures support on-the-job training (see section on Developing Human Resources for Investment) • How does the government support technology and knowledge transfer between companies (see section on *Investment Policy*)? • What measures are in place to promote the internationalisation of SMEs (see section on *Trade Policy*)?
International and regional networks to promote investment	• Does the government use its own, broader international network, such as its diplomatic representation, to promote investment? Are there dedicated trade and investment officers posted in key embassies? How is co-ordination with the capital ensured? • To what extent is investment promotion undertaken at the regional level, involving members of the same regional economic grouping? • Is the national investment promotion strategy implemented in partnership with sub-national entities (i.e. with provincial/regional/local IPAs) so as to avoid investor fatigue and costly duplication of efforts? • Has the government made use of international and regional initiatives aimed at building investment promotion expertise? Has the investment promotion agency joined regional and international networks?

Additional resources

Websites

OECD Investment, *www.oecd.org/investment/.*

Global Enterprise Registration, *http://ger.co/.*

PublicPrivateDialogue.org, *www.publicprivatedialogue.org.*

SME Toolkit, *www.smetoolkit.org.*

Subcontracting and Partnership Exchange, *www.unido.org/spx.*

World Association of Investment Promotion Agencies, official website, *www.waipa.org* World Bank Group, Investment generation toolkit, *www.wbginvestmentclimate.org/toolkits/investment-generation-toolkit/.*

Tools, guidance, manuals

The E-regulations System, *www.theiguides.org/media/website/The_EREGULATIONS_SYSTEM_brochure.pdf.*

Millennium Cities Initiative and Vale Columbia Center (2009), *Handbook for Promoting Foreign Direct Investment in Medium-Size, Low Budget Cities in Emerging Markets*, Millennium Cities Initiative, New York.

OECD (2011), *Attractiveness for Innovation: Location Factors for International Investment*, OECD Publishing, Paris, *http://dx.doi.org/10.1787/9789264104815-en.*

OECD (2007), *Competitive Regional Clusters: National Policy Approaches*, OECD Reviews of Regional Innovation, OECD Publishing, Paris, *http://dx.doi.org/10.1787/9789264031838-en.*

OECD-WTO-World Bank (2014), *Global Value Chains: Challenges, Opportunities and Implications for Policy.*

UNCTAD (2010), *Creating Business Linkages: A Policy Perspective*, United Nations Conference for Trade and Development, Geneva.

UNCTAD (2008), *Evaluating Investment Promotion Agencies*, United Nations Conference for Trade and Development, Geneva.

UNCTAD (2007), *Aftercare: A Core Function in Investment Promotion*, United Nations Conference for Trade and Development, Geneva.

UNCTAD (2007), *Investment Promotion Agency as Policy Advocates*, United Nations Conference for Trade and Development, Geneva.

UNIDO (2011), *Africa Investor Report 2011*, United Nations Industrial Development Organisation, Vienna.

UNIDO (2003), *Guidelines for Investment Promotion Agencies: Foreign Direct Investment Flows to Developing Countries*, United Nations Industrial Development Organisation, Vienna.

World Bank (2012), *Global Investment Promotion Best Practices 2012*, World Bank Group, Washington, DC.

World Bank (2009), *Global Investment Promotion Benchmarking 2009: Summary Report*, World Bank Group, Washington, DC.

World Bank (2008), *Special Economic Zones: Performance, Lessons Learned, and Implications for Zone Development (2008)*, World Bank Group, Washington, DC.

World Bank (2004), *The Effectiveness of Promotion Agencies at Attracting Foreign Direct Investment*, FIAS Occasional Paper, World Bank Group, Washington, DC.

World Bank (2003), *Does a country need a promotion agency to attract foreign direct investment? A small analytical model applied to 58 countries*, Policy Research Working Paper, World Bank Group, Washington, DC.

World Bank (2000), *Marketing a Country: Promotion as a Tool for Attracting Foreign Investment*, FIAS Occasional Paper, World Bank Group, Washington, DC.

Indicators

World Bank, *Ease of Doing Business Indicators*, *www.doingbusiness.org.*

AT Kearney, *Global Services Location Index*, *www.atkearney.com/research-studies/global-services-location-index.*

Policy Framework for Investment
2015 Edition

3. Trade policy

Trade policies influence the size of markets for the output of firms and hence can shape both foreign and domestic investment. Over time, the influence of trade policies on the investment climate is growing. Changes in technology, liberalisation of host country policies towards trade and investment and the growing importance of trade within global production chains have all served to make trade policy an important ingredient in encouraging both foreign and domestic investment and in maximising the contribution of that investment to development.

Trade liberalising measures, undertaken unilaterally or as part of binding multilateral and preferential trade and investment agreements, can improve allocative efficiency, provide access to larger markets, allow for greater scale economies and hence lower costs.

Open, predictable and transparent trade and investment policies are also necessary to remain competitive in a world where global value chains (GVCs) are a dominant feature of world trade. More than one half of world manufacturing imports and 70% of service imports are intermediate goods and services. When production is fragmented in this way and goods and services cross borders many times, tariffs, non-tariff barriers and other restrictive measures affect not only foreign suppliers, but also domestic producers (see questions on linkages in the section on *Investment Promotion and Facilitation*). Fast and efficient customs and border procedures and well-functioning transport, logistics, finance, communication and other business and professional services are particularly important. Open trade and investment regimes, including streamlined and efficient customs procedures help ensure that inputs are competitively priced and that trade costs are reduced.

Ensuring that trade policies and practices contribute fully to a favourable investment climate also requires the same emphasis on transparency, policy stability and predictability, public consultations and periodic evaluation and review found in other policy areas and described in the opening section to the PFI. Governments additionally need to ensure that customs, and trade-related regulatory and administrative procedures are no more burdensome than necessary to achieve their stated policy objectives while reducing transaction costs for firms. The speed and ease of trading goods and services across borders has a direct impact on the attractiveness of particular economies and industries to investors, particularly in the context of regional and global value chains.

Governments sometimes use trade policy instruments, such as import tariffs (including tariff peaks and escalating tariffs) and other measures (such as local content requirements, exports restrictions), to promote investment in targeted industries. But the growing interdependence of economies, as well as the sectoral linkages within economies (for example the role of quality services to support a competitive manufacturing sector), requires a keener awareness on the part of policy-makers of the costs and benefits of using trade policy to achieve objectives that other, more efficient policy instruments may be suitably equipped to pursue in the areas of labour market, education, innovation and SME development policies.

Home country policies

Beyond offering reciprocal market access through trade agreements, the international community can contribute in other areas of trade policy to improving the quantity and quality of investment in a given country. For least developed countries, preferential access to larger markets through eased access for their goods and services can foster their participation in global trade.

Governments can also provide assistance to a given country, via aid for trade and other assistance, to help its firms comply with sanitary, phytosanitary and other standards, build capacity to negotiate and implement trade agreements, address other supply side constraints that affect the trading environment and market failures related to trade finance and credit insurance and guarantees. Markets that facilitate cross-border transactions, including those that hedge against risks attached to exchange rate movements and payment defaults as well as those for transit insurance and export finance, can all enhance both trade and investment.

Core questions and principles

1. What recent efforts has the government undertaken to reduce the compliance costs of customs, regulatory and other administrative procedures at the border?
2. To what extent has the government addressed behind the border barriers to trade, particularly services or regulations?
3. Has the government evaluated how trade policies can be applied to facilitate the participation of local firms in global value chains, particularly through lowering the costs of inputs?
4. How actively is the government increasing investment opportunities through market-expanding international trade agreements and ensuring consistency of its policies with its WTO commitments?
5. Does the government use trade policy to favour investment in some industries and discourage it in others? How are these policies reviewed with a view to reducing the costs associated with these distortions? What effort does the government make to ensure that such policies are consistent with the country's commitments in the WTO and other international trade agreements?
6. Does the government benefit from market access for its exports, and does it help leverage that access so that export prospects encourage domestic and foreign investment in that country? Is aid for trade available and does the government promote appropriate conditions to leverage the aid for trade provided to assist in addressing supply side constraints to taking advantage of market access opportunities?
7. How do home countries help to address market failures which might inhibit exports from developing or emerging economies (e.g. export finance, working capital, and import insurance)?

Supplemental questions

Trade facilitation measures	What has the government done to reduce transaction costs for firms engaging in trade by: • Simplifying and increasing transparency and predictability of customs and other border procedures? • Using risk-management techniques to optimise border control (selectivity criteria and post-clearance audits)? • Introducing electronic customs clearance systems and Single Windows for Trade? • Harmonising and simplifying documents and streamlining procedures? • Using periodic audits of regulations or built-in sunset clauses to take account of changed contexts? • Performing ex ante reviews of proposed regulations and consulting with stakeholders to ensure their optimal design? • Applying internationally-agreed standards and streamlining conformity assessment procedures? • Co-operating with regional and international peers?
Services and other regulations	• What has the government done to reduce services barriers to trade? • In what specific services sectors have barriers been reduced? • Has the government raised barriers to trade in services; if so in what sectors? • Does the government ensure that regulatory measures are (i) based on objective and transparent criteria such as competence and the ability to supply the service, (ii) not more burdensome than necessary to ensure the quality of services and (iii) in the case of licensing procedures, are not in themselves a restriction on the supply of the services? Has the government entered into agreements with other governments to co-operate on regulations that affect trade? See also questions on regulatory reform in the section on *Public Governance.*
Trade liberalisation and international trade agreements	• How important is multilateral, regional and unilateral liberalisation of goods and services in the government's strategy to increase market opportunities? • How is the government increasing capacity and resources to negotiate and implement trade agreements? • To what extent does the government consult with stakeholders on proposed trade reforms? • Does the government evaluate in advance the costs and benefits associated with entering the legal commitments present in international trade agreements (see the questions on international investment agreements in the section on *Investment Policy*)? • What does the government do to help business, particularly SMEs, to identify and pursue trade and investment opportunities opened up through trade agreements?
Trade promotion	• Does the government have a mechanism to assess impediments to exports of local firms and the means of addressing them? Is there the same mechanism for imports? How do government programmes support the objective of diversification of sourcing- and export products and markets? • What does the government do to foster co-operation between investment and trade promotion agencies, especially by providing various forms of market intelligence to SMEs? • How does the government identify capacity-building priorities in relevant government ministries and agencies and direct attention to the capacity development needs of SMEs? • How does the government assist domestic enterprises to conform to standards in key export markets, including sanitary and phytosanitary (SPS) requirements? • Does it help businesses benefit from trade and investment promotion activities, such as through participation in trade fairs?
Targeted trade policies	• To what extent does the government use import tariffs, local content requirements, export restrictions or other trade-related policies to promote investment in targeted industries? • On what basis are these sectors selected? • Does the government engage in public consultations when deciding on policies to promote or protect particular sectors? • Does the government assess whether the policies implemented actually meet the identified policy objectives? Does the government assess whether these policies are consistent with the country's commitments in the WTO and other international trade agreements, particularly in the case of local content requirements? • Does the government assess the impact of these policies on the competitiveness of other sectors which rely on these imports as inputs for their own exports, as well as on the overall investment climate? • Does the government make use of regulatory impact assessments for these purposes? • Does the government consider alternative methods of promoting industrial development in priority sectors which would not discriminate against foreign competitors? See section on *Investment Policy* on non-discrimination, section on *Competition Policy* on the competitive implications of industrial policies and section on *Public Governance* on regulatory impact assessments.
Global value chains	• What efforts has the government undertaken to foster the participation of local firms in global value chains? • Does the government offer duty exemptions on imported inputs? • Does the government measure the importance of intermediate inputs, including services, in overall exports and the effective rates of protection in these sectors? • Has the government evaluated how services trade policies could help firms enter global value chains through lowering entry costs. See section on *Investment Promotion and Facilitation* for a discussion of how to increase local value addition and linkages with local firms, including SMEs.

International co-operation	• Does the country have duty-free, quota-free access to trading partners? To which countries? For which exports? What actions and policies has the country deployed to leverage such DFQF schemes? • Does the country have any other form of preferential access to the markets of its trading partners? To which countries? For which exports? What action and policies has the country deployed to leverage such preferential access? • Where trading partners apply SPS, TBT or other regulatory requirements, what actions and polices are carried out to best utilise any assistance provided to meet those requirements? • Is the government able to access aid for trade to help address supply side constraints to trade? In what specific areas? Does the government promote appropriate conditions to leverage the aid for trade provided?
For importing countries	• Does the importing country government consider external costs on trading partners when evaluating domestic trade policy measures? • How can domestic policy makers safeguard the need of regulatory authorities to address legitimate domestic policy objectives without recourse to needlessly burdensome trade measures? • Does the government fulfil the requirements of the WTO Technical Barriers to Trade and SPS Agreement in terms of not making regulatory measures more trade restrictive than necessary? • Do specific provisions exist in the context of an RIA that would require or encourage regulators to avoid unnecessary trade restrictiveness with a view to minimising potentially adverse effects on trading partners?
Export finance and risk mitigation	• How does the government ensure adequacy of available trade finance solutions for local firms interested in trade opportunities? • Do local financial institutions participate in the World Bank's Global Trade Finance Programme and/or the trade finance programs of regional development banks? • Do they take advantage of trade finance training opportunities?

Additional resources

Websites

OECD, *Trade Facilitation, www.oecd.org/trade/facilitation.*

OECD, *Global Value Chains, www.oecd.org/industry/ind/global-value-chains.htm.*

World Customs Organisation, *www.wcoomd.org.*

WTO, Working Group on Trade, Debt and Finance, World Trade Organisation *www.wto.org/english/thewto_e/coher_e/tr_finance_e.htm.*

Principles, standards

WCO (1974), *Kyoto Convention on the Simplification and Harmonisation of Customs Procedures,* World Customs Organisation, Brussels.

WTO, *Agreement on Technical Barriers to Trade*, World Trade Organisation, Geneva.

APEC (2001), *APEC Principles on Trade Facilitation*, Asia-Pacific Economic Co-operation, Singapore.

Publications

OECD (2014), "Global value chains in Africa: Potential and evidence", in AfDB, OECD/UNDP, *African Economic Outlook 2014: Global Value Chains and Africa's Industrialisation*, OECD Publishing, Paris, *http://dx.doi.org/10.1787/aeo-2014-9-en.*

OECD (2013), *Interconnected Economies: Benefiting from Global Value Chains,* OECD Publishing, Paris, *http://dx.doi.org/10.1787/9789264189560-en.*

OECD (2008), *Enhancing the Role of SMEs in Global Value Chains*, OECD Publishing, Paris, *http://dx.doi.org/10.1787/9789264051034-en.*

OECD, WTO, UNCTAD (2013), *Implications of Global Value Chains for Trade, Investment, Development and Jobs, www.oecd.org/sti/ind/G20-Global-Value-Chains-2013.pdf.*

OECD, WTO and World Bank (2014), *Global Value Chains: Challenges, Opportunities and Implications for Policy, www.oecd.org/tad/gvc_report_g20_july_2014.pdf.*

UNCTAD (2013), *Global Value Chains: Investment and Trade for Development*, United Nations Conference for Trade and Development, UNCTAD, Geneva.

Tools, guidance, manuals

World Bank (2006), *Reforming the Regulation Procedures for Import and Export: Guide for Practitioners,* World Bank Group, Washington, DC.

APEC (2005), *APEC Customs and Trade Facilitation Handbook*, Asia-Pacific Economic Co-operation, Singapore

ADB (2013), *Designing and Implementing Trade Facilitation in Asia and the Pacific*, Asian Development Bank, Manila.

Indicators, benchmarking

OECD, *Services Trade Restrictiveness Index*, *www.oecd.org/tad/services-trade/services-trade-restrictiveness-index.htm.*

OECD, *Trade Facilitation Indicators*, *www.oecd.org/trade/facilitation/indicators.htm.*

WCO (2011), *Time Release Study*, World Customs Organisation, Brussels.

WCO, *Customs International Benchmarking Manual*, World Customs Organisation, Brussels.

World Bank, "Trading across Borders", Ease of Doing Business Indicators, *www.doing business.org.*

Policy Framework for Investment
2015 Edition

4. Competition policy

Effective competition is essential for a dynamic business environment in which firms are willing to take risks and invest.

A competitive environment encourages risk-taking and, thus, investment. There is, in addition, extensive empirical evidence that industries facing greater competition experience faster productivity growth, because competition allows more efficient firms to enter and gain market share at the expense of less efficient ones. In competitive markets firms succeed when they better satisfy their consumers. Furthermore, without competition there is little incentive to innovate. Newer products and processes allow firms to get ahead of the game. An environment of productivity growth, innovation and business success – to which competition typically contributes – is one conducive to investor confidence and, therefore, investment.

Creating and maintaining a competitive environment requires a sound and well-structured competition law, an effective competition authority that enforces this law, and, more widely, economic policies that respect the principles of competition and avoid unnecessarily restricting it.

A sound competition law guarantees that firms know "the rules of the game" and respect them. Such a law should prohibit anticompetitive vertical and horizontal agreements, as well as exclusionary practices by dominant companies, and it should provide for the review of mergers and acquisitions to prevent the creation of conditions that can lead to a reduction in competition. As a guiding principle, the rules should apply equally to all firms – whether private or state-owned, foreign or domestic – in all sectors, and exemptions should exist only when absolutely necessary and well-justified.

Even a well-designed competition law can be effective only if it is properly enforced. An adequately resourced, skilled and independent competition authority is needed, which fulfils its mandate free from any political interference. The agency should have the necessary power and tools to uncover illegal practices and to impose sanctions for infringements, so as to ensure a reasonable level of deterrence, while being proportionate. It should also provide confidence in a fair and transparent application of the law, by guaranteeing the right to a fair process, clarity about the rules and consistency and predictability in their enforcement, certainty about the length of the enforcement procedures, and protection of confidential information. Ambiguous rules and non-transparent proceedings of unpredictable duration do not foster a climate of trust and certainty, and discourage firms from investing.

Deterring and stopping anticompetitive behaviour and anticompetitive mergers is a necessary, but not sufficient, condition for ensuring a competitive environment. Other economic policies have to contribute to achieve this aim.

Sometimes competition can be weakened by other government interventions pursuing different objectives. To avoid this outcome, government and public bodies should systematically assess the impact on competition of proposed policies, laws and regulations, and should eliminate any unnecessary obstacles and distortions to competition these may create, unless essential to the achievement of other policy goals. Competition agencies should seek to use their expertise and knowledge to provide advice and support. Competition agencies can contribute by identifying on their own initiative any distortions to competition introduced by government interventions.

Similarly the principles of fair and effective competition should inform how the public sector procures its goods and services and awards concessions for the provision of services using public resources. Competitive tendering based on clear, transparent, and non-discriminatory rules should be used to select the best providers, and any form of bid-rigging should be detected and punished.

Privatisation and liberalisation policies should be designed so as to promote the entry of new players and sustainable and effective competition. This may include accounting or functional separation, and in some cases even structural separation when necessary to separate the competitive and non-competitive elements of the industry and to avoid discrimination and cross-subsidisation. Appropriate sectoral regulation has to be introduced, in order to balance the need to avoid the incumbent exploiting its advantages to foreclose entry and expansion, and the need to provide new and existing industry players (including incumbents) with the proper incentives to invest. Liberalisation, when properly implemented, is considered to have an unambiguously positive effect on investment.

The questions listed in the rest of this section are meant as a guide for policy makers to determine if, and to what extent, these pillars are in place in a given country, and how laws, policies and institutions can be improved to create the appropriate environment to foster competition and hence favour investment.

Core questions and principles

1. Do you have an independent and -adequately resourced competition authority with the necessary powers to enforce competition law effectively?
2. Are any exemptions to the application of competition law limited and justified?
3. Do you have a competition law that prohibits anticompetitive agreements, and anticompetitive conduct by dominant companies, and that provides the necessary tools to uncover such illegal practices, as well as adequate sanctions to deter them?
4. Does your competition law provide for the review of mergers and acquisitions that can harm competition?
5. Does your competition law provide for a fair and transparent process to the parties involved in competition investigations and proceedings, and for effective judicial review?
6. Are the effects on competition of policies, laws and regulations considered and any unnecessary impediments to competition removed?
7. Has sectoral economic regulation been imposed only when necessary and proportionate?
8. Does the public procurement regime ensure a level playing field among companies competing for contracts and guarantee that the best value offer is selected?

Supplemental questions

Independence of the competition authority	• Is the competition authority independent? To whom does the authority report? How is it financed? • If there are other authorities, e.g. sectoral regulators, that have the responsibility to protect or foster competition, are their respective roles and areas of interest well-defined, so as to avoid conflicting interventions?
Exemptions to competition law	• Are there sectors or economic actors (e.g. state-owned enterprises or small and medium enterprises) that are partially or fully exempt from the application of competition law? • Is there an economic rationale or a public interest rationale for these exemptions?
Addressing anticompetitive practices	• Does your competition law prohibit hard core cartel agreements and other anticompetitive horizontal or vertical agreements? • Does your competition law prohibit abuses of dominant position/monopolisation? • When the competition authority assesses whether an agreement or a unilateral behaviour is anticompetitive, does it only consider the impact these may have on competition, or are other factors (e.g. impact on employment) also taken into account? • Is the determination of whether a firm holds a dominant position in a market based on solid economic criteria? • Does the competition agency have the necessary power and tools to uncover such illegal practices (e.g. inspection powers)? • Does the competition law permit the imposition of sanctions for infringements of the competition law that are adequate to ensure a reasonable level of deterrence, while being proportionate? • Is there a leniency program to help uncover cartels?
Mergers and acquisitions	• Does your competition law require the review of mergers and acquisitions by the competition agency before they are completed? • Is there a threshold for notification that limits the scrutiny of the competition authority to the more economically relevant mergers and acquisitions? • Are there statutory timetables that provide certainty about the duration of merger and acquisition reviews? • Can the companies involved propose remedies to address any competition concern raised by a merger or acquisition? • Are there special, more restrictive criteria for assessing mergers and acquisitions that involve foreign companies? • Can a merger be *blocked* or allowed on grounds other than its effects on competition?
Competition enforcement	• Are the competition rules and practices that regulate competition enforcement public and accessible to all interested parties? • Does your legislation provide procedural fairness to companies investigated by the competition authority with the right to a due process (e.g. notice of the reasons for the investigation, a right to be heard and to present evidence, opportunities to meet with the authority, etc.)? • Are there protections for ensuring that confidential or privileged business information provided by companies during investigations, merger reviews and market studies is not disclosed to third parties? • Does your legislation allow for competition authority decisions to be effectively reviewed by an independent appellate body? • Does your legal system allow for compensation of the victims of competition law infringements (e.g. accessible procedures to seek damages for the losses they have incurred)?
Effects of policies, laws and regulations on competition	• Does the competition authority have the power to undertake market studies in markets where competition does not appear to be effective and propose recommendations to address any impediment to competition it may identify? • Do the government/ministries regularly assess the impact on competition of proposed policies (including direct and indirect subsidies), laws and regulations that may have implications for competition (e.g. those that restrict entry, access, exit, pricing, output, normal commercial practices, and forms of business organisation) and consider alternative arrangements to meet the same objectives with less distortive effect on competition? • Is the competition authority involved in this process (e.g. performs the assessments, provides advice)? • Has the competition authority been involved in the design of privatisation processes?
Sectoral economic regulation	• Are natural monopolies, whether state-owned or private, regulated to ensure that prices are not excessive, and do they have incentives to reduce costs? • When a legal monopoly has been opened to competition (liberalisation), has appropriate regulation been imposed on the incumbent to ensure that competition can develop? • Are there measures to ensure co-ordination and consistency between competition law enforcement and economic sectoral regulation?
Competition and public procurement	• Are public authorities required to guarantee transparency, equal treatment and non-discrimination when procuring goods and services or awarding concessions? • Are tenders designed to ensure that only value for money bids are selected? • Can sanctions be imposed for engaging in bid rigging activities that ensure an adequate level of deterrence?

Additional resources

OECD, *Competition policy*, *www.oecd.org/daf/competition/*.

OECD (2014), *Competition and macroeconomic outcomes factsheet*, *www.oecd.org/daf/competition/factsheet-macroeconomics-competition.htm*.

OECD (2001), *Recommendation concerning Structural Separation in Regulated Industries*, *www. oecd.org/daf/competition/recommendationconcerningstructuralseparationinregulatedindustries.htm*.

OECD, *Competition Assessment Toolkit*, *www.oecd.org/daf/competition/assessment-toolkit.htm*.

OECD, *Country reviews of competition policy frameworks*, *www.oecd.org/daf/competition/countryreviewsofcompetitionpolicyframeworks.htm*.

OECD, *Fighting bid rigging in public procurement*, *www.oecd.org/daf/competition/fightingbid rigginginpublicprocurement.htm*.

OECD, *Pro-competitive Policy Reforms*, *www.oecd.org/daf/competition/reforms/*.

Policy Framework for Investment
2015 Edition

5. Tax policy

Tax policy to support development objectives and investment attraction strategies

Investment promotion authorities and revenue collection agencies often have shared responsibilities, but are working towards different objectives, especially in the developing country context. Policy makers should take a holistic view of their country's tax rates and tax mix to balance the broad range of social and development objectives against the need to attract investment. Investment promotion agencies feel compelled to offer tax incentives in order to attract investors, while tax policy-makers and revenue collection agencies argue that revenues need to be raised to provide public goods, including the key pillars of a business-enabling environment, such as infrastructure and a healthy and educated workforce. Effective co-ordination of tax policy makers with various authorities that are mandated to promote investment, including at local government levels is a daunting but critically important task. One feature of those countries that have been successful in designing tax policy attractive to investment, is that they have generally adopted a whole-of-government approach to ensure consistency between the country's tax policy, its broader national and sub-national development objectives and its overall investment attraction strategy.

Policy makers should regularly assess the tax burden on profits to determine if the tax system is conducive to the type of investment the country seeks to attract. The main statutory provisions as well as the effects of tax-planning strategies increasingly used by businesses to lower the tax burden should be taken into account. Compliance costs from excessive complexity, a lack of transparency and unpredictability in the tax system should also be considered. If the tax burden on business income is judged to be inappropriate, either too high to attract and retain investment or too low in relation to the country's revenue needs, consideration should be given to adjusting the statutory tax parameters.

Commonly used tax burden measures vary in terms of relevance, data intensity and complexity of use. When considering investment options investors analyse the entire tax landscape, but often their first point of reference is the ***statutory tax rate*** – perhaps the most visible tax measure in consideration of potential investment. Statutory corporate rates carry an important signal function and are commonly used in cross-country comparisons by global investors, but statutory tax rates are limited in their ability to reflect the whole tax landscape in the country. Indeed, ***effective tax rates***, that capture specific provisions of the tax legislation, such as tax incentives to promote investment, are better indicators of the tax system's burden on businesses and the incentives to invest. Policy analysts utilise backward-looking and forward-looking effective tax burden measures. When micro-level firm-specific data is available for analysis, backward-looking average effective tax rates are arguably the best measures of the tax burden of the corporate sector, as they reflect actual (not hypothetical) business activities. Forward-looking effective tax rate indicators, such as marginal effective tax rates (METR) and average effective tax rates (AETR) capture the net effect of basic statutory tax provisions on a hypothetical investment project. METRs summarise the effect of the legislative tax parameters on an incremental business activity and show how much to invest on the margin given a diminishing expected return on investment. AETRs are a more general tax burden indicator that assesses the impact of taxation on an investor, such as a typical multinational enterprise, when it is weighing up its investment decisions in relation to two or more competing projects.

The advantage of using effective tax rates is that they combine complex information about the statutory tax rate, the level and type of depreciation allowances, the years of reduced tax rates or even tax holidays, and any special investment allowances, into a *single* measure. This measure expresses the tax liability as a share of the present value of all financial profits expected from an investment. The effective tax rate therefore is based on many factors, including the expected rate of profitability, the type of assets invested in (because depreciation allowances differ across buildings and plants and machinery), and the type of financing used (because of interest deductibility). It can be negative because, for some investments, the tax advantages can be greater than profits.

Impact of tax policy on investment decisions

Despite analysis indicating limited investment response to a lower tax burden relative to revenue forgone, tax incentives are routinely chosen by governments to attract investment in general, and foreign direct investment (FDI) in particular. The rationale behind this widespread practice is obvious, particularly in the context of developing countries. It is much easier to provide tax incentives than to correct deficiencies in, for example, infrastructure or skilled labour. Tax incentives do not require an actual expenditure of funds or cash subsidies to investors and are politically easier to provide than public funds. Moreover, there is some merit to the arguments used by politicians and policy makers to justify their decisions to offer tax incentives in order to attract investment. Indeed, domestic savings, especially in emerging and developing countries, could be so low and financial intermediation so weak, that they are insufficient to finance economic expansion, effectively limiting business resources for investment. In such environments, a lower tax burden is thought to attract FDI as a source of external finance. Further, evidence suggests that investment may generate positive externalities – "spillovers" – toward the host economy. Investment can act as a trigger for technology and know-how transfers, facilitate the upgrading of workers' skills and improved human capital formation, assist enterprise development and restructuring, nurture business clusters and contribute to deeper international (trade) integration.

A country's tax burden is one of many, and not always the most important, factor considered by potential investors when weighing up investment decisions. Critically important to potential investors are questions over costs and risks associated with macroeconomic and business conditions, the cost of compliance with laws, regulations and administrative practices, market size, labour-force conditions, and above all, location-specific profit opportunities. For certain types of investment, the levels of profit and risk associated with undertaking a given business activity may require a physical presence in a particular location and cannot be realised by locating in another country or jurisdiction. Location specific activities may include investing in infrastructure and utilities (such as transport, communications and power supply), the extraction of natural resources and the provision of restaurant and hotel services. Where an economy offers an abundance of location-specific profit opportunities, policy makers may understandably resist pressures to adopt a relatively low tax burden to protect their revenue base. Further, a higher host country tax burden could generally be acceptable to investors if the country offers attractive business conditions, a stable macroeconomic framework, a stable tax policy environment, the rule of law, a well-trained labour force, regulatory certainty, and effective investment promotion systems (the latter are discussed in detail under the sections on *Investment Policy* and *Investment Promotion and Facilitation*).

In the context of economic profit that is not location-specific, comparisons of the country's actual tax burden with those of competing jurisdictions are expected to be taken into account. If a given business activity can be carried out in a competing location with a lower rate than that in the host country, then, in theory, investors would be unwilling to bear a tax burden in the host country above that rate. A country's tax burden that is very high relative to competitor countries would generally discourage investment and could, in certain cases, be a deciding factor for not investing or reinvesting in a particular country. However, measures to lower a country's tax burden vis-à-vis its competitor jurisdictions can potentially lead to a "race to the bottom", making countries collectively worse off. This is of particular concern in developing countries where often new measures are introduced or existing measures are significantly augmented without properly assessing the likely reactions of other jurisdictions. This issue cannot be tackled in isolation; governments need to work together on a regional basis to increase co-operation in the area of tax.

Prudent use of tax incentives

Tax systems may impose a non-uniform effective tax rate on different businesses, depending on their size, ownership structure (e.g. domestic versus foreign-owned), business activity or location. Certain firms may be specifically targeted to receive preferential tax treatment. In some cases, there might indeed be good reasons for implementing targeted tax incentives. Where tax relief is targeted, policy makers should examine and weigh arguments in favour of and against such treatment, and ensure that the different treatment can be properly justified. The standard justification for differential tax treatment on efficiency grounds is that tax incentives can correct for market imperfections. These "market correction" arguments are based on the assumptions that private investors do not take into account the benefits to the larger society of certain types of investment, such as for example renewable energy development, which leads to under-investment. Another market failure argument suggests that asymmetric information on markets or products or monopoly power of large firms could make entry difficult for SMEs or make it difficult for SMEs to raise finance. The administrative argument is that it is often easier for governments to administer a tax incentives programme than to deliver a similarly-targeted expenditure programme. Some investment incentives have redistributive goals, for example, policies aimed at increasing investment and bolstering employment and growth in poorer parts of a country.

Tax burden measures that vary considerably from one investment type to another must be explained. Policy makers want to know whether their targeted investment approach is effective in meeting its intended policy objectives (e.g. encourage investment in disadvantaged regions). Beyond this, efficient targeting requires accurate estimates of the amount of tax revenue forgone in order to compare the realised benefit against the costs associated with the targeted incentives. Further considerations in targeting tax incentives involve containing tax relief to targeted firms/activities only (e.g. to small businesses).

Evaluating costs and benefits of tax incentives

If a tax incentive programme is to contribute to a country's economic welfare, its benefits should exceed its costs. It is therefore important that decision makers have a capacity to distinguish between beneficial and wasteful tax incentive programmes. As such, thorough analysis of the effectiveness and cost-efficiency of proposed tax incentives should be conducted both prior to the introduction of investment-promotion measures as well as systematically ex-post, to assess the extent to which, and the cost at which tax incentives meet their intended objectives.

An evaluation of the economic ***benefits*** of tax incentives should take into account a) direct impact by the incentives-motivated investment; b) indirect and induced impact due to inter-industry transactions and changes in income and consumption; c) positive externalities, such as technology and know-how transfers by incentives-induced FDI; and d) social and environmental benefits where tax incentives serve to correct market imperfections. The **costs** that should be considered when conducting a cost-benefit analysis of a given tax incentives programme include; a) primary revenue forgone due to tax incentives; b) revenue leakages due to unintended and unforeseen tax-planning opportunities; c) costs incurred by taxpayers in order to comply with a given tax incentives regime; d) the administrative costs from running the tax incentives programmes due to the complexity introduced to the legislative and regulatory framework; and e) the costs to the economy of creating an "uneven playing field" where domestic firms are not entitled to the same tax incentives as their foreign competitors.

Transparency and good governance of tax incentives systems

In creating an investment-promoting business environment, the issues of transparency and clarity in the provisions of tax incentives are of key importance. In this respect, selective tax incentive programmes in which authorities have a great deal of discretion increase an investor's uncertainty about how the tax system will treat them in comparison with their competitors and may inadvertently discourage, rather than encourage, investment. A poorly designed tax system, where the rules and their application lack transparency, are overly complex or unpredictable, may add to project costs and uncertainty. Excessive administrative discretion in the hands of tax officials can seriously increase the risk of corruption and undermine good governance objectives fundamental to securing an attractive investment environment. Additionally, any provisions over which tax authorities have discretion as to their application create opportunities for rent-seeking as firms try to "convince" authorities to approve their applications for benefits. As such, general tax incentives and those that involve little or no discretion in their application are preferred to the ones that involve government decision making in picking "winners and losers".

The granting of tax incentives for investment in developing countries can often be done outside of a country's tax laws and administration, sometimes under multiple pieces of legislation. The design and administration of tax incentives may be the responsibility of several different Ministries (e.g. finance, trade, investment). Where various Ministries are involved, they may not coordinate their incentive measures with each other or the national revenue authority, with the result that incentives may overlap, be inconsistent, or even work at cross-purposes.

In many developing countries, tax incentives could be provided through the tax laws (e.g. income tax law), but could also be provided through laws governing investment, Special

Economic Zones, etc.; in other cases, the incentives regime may be established through decrees, agreements and regulations that exist outside of the tax law. As a result the true extent of tax incentives that may be available can be hidden. Consolidating all tax incentives, along with their eligibility criteria, into the main body of the tax law, increases transparency and may remove any doubt that the tax administration is empowered to administer them.

Countering abusive tax planning strategies domestically and internationally

Tax incentives, depending on their type and design, can give rise to certain unintended and unwelcome results. Policy makers must recognise that all taxpayers will analyse the targeting criteria and attempt to benefit from the tax incentive. For example, experience shows that a non-qualifying (medium or large) firm may reorganise itself into two or more new business entities to attempt to access tax relief conditional on firm size. Similarly, companies will attempt to characterise or re-characterise certain activities so that they fall within the boundaries of qualifying business activities, for example, to qualify for R&D tax incentives. Tax holidays or partial profit exemptions, in particular, offer significant scope for aggressive tax planning. These incentives are typically targeted at "new" companies, but old firms commonly reconstitute as "new" ones towards the end of their holiday periods, so that they can continue to be tax-exempt. Further, partial or full profit exemption also opens up transfer pricing opportunities to artificially shift taxable income from non-qualifying business entities to entities that do qualify. Non-qualifying companies can channel asset purchases through qualifying companies. Likewise, qualifying firms in a loss position may attempt to sell their balances of unused business losses and tax credits to profitable firms outside the target tax incentive group so that these firms may reduce their tax liability. Inevitably, the government can come under pressure to extend tax incentive relief to taxpayers/activities that were not initially targeted.

Core questions and principles

1. How does the government's tax policy support its development objectives and its investment attraction strategy?
2. Given the socio-economic and political conditions of the country, is it reasonable to assume that policy, including tax incentives can favourably affect investment decisions?
3. Where tax incentives are targeted to special groups/locations, can a non-uniform treatment of investors be justified?
4. Does appraisal of costs and benefits of tax incentives regularly take place to support government decision-making?
5. Are tax incentives consolidated in the tax law? Are they offered on an automatic or discretionary basis? Is the process for granting and administering tax incentives clear and transparent?
6. Have unintended domestic and cross-border tax-planning opportunities been evaluated? Have measures been taken to improve international tax co-operation to counter abusive tax planning strategies?

Supplemental questions

Consistency of tax policy with broader development strategy	• Does the government have a coherent tax policy in line with its broader development objectives and its investment attraction strategy? • Is the prevailing tax policy developed and amended through a whole-of-government approach that effectively balances the domestic revenue mobilisation and investment attraction priorities of the government? • What is the average current tax burden on domestic profits? Has the assessment of the actual tax burden taken into account statutory provisions as well as tax-planning opportunities and compliance costs? • Is the tax burden on business enterprises appropriate with reference to the government's broader policy goals and investment attraction objectives? • Are the main tax provisions generally consistent with international norms and reasonable expectations of investors? • Has the government identified the elements of the country's tax system that significantly distort investment choices and discourage entrepreneurial activity?
Understanding potential effect of tax incentives on investment	• Has the government analysed the strengths and weaknesses of its business climate? Given the socio-economic, institutional, and political conditions of the country, does a lower tax burden have the potential to impact favourably on investment decisions? • Has the government critically evaluated if existing or proposed tax incentives programmes are the right policy instruments to stimulate investment? • What alternative measures to address the country's priorities have been evaluated? Is the fiscal burden of alternative policy instruments comparable with the fiscal burden of a given/proposed tax incentives programme? • If and when tax incentives are deemed to be beneficial vis-à-vis the country's most pressing priorities, what considerations are taken into account in designing an effective tax incentives programme? • Has the government critically assessed the impact of the existing or proposed tax incentives policies on competing jurisdictions?
Prudent use of targeted tax incentives	• Are tax incentives applied uniformly to all investors or are they targeted to special groups/locations? • Are there special groups/locations where higher than standard tax rates apply? • Can a non-uniform treatment of investors be justified? Has the government assessed whether the targeted investment approach is effective in meeting its intended policy objectives? • Is the tax system neutral in its treatment of foreign and domestic investors? • Is the tax system tailored to the specific circumstances of small business? If yes, is the special treatment justified? Is it effective in meeting its intended policy goals? • Has the government examined distortions to investment decisions introduced by the targeted tax incentives? • Has the government evaluated tax planning opportunities resulting from non-uniform tax treatment of targeted activities? • What considerations have been made to contain tax relief to targeted firms/activities?
Evaluation of costs and benefits of tax incentives	• Are tax incentives monitored and evaluated to analyse their effectiveness to support government decision-making? • Are mechanisms established to regularly assess the costs and benefits of tax incentives for investment? • What data are collected to assess the effectiveness and cost-efficiency of individual tax incentives? Are mechanisms established to collect data systematically? • Are "benefits" of tax incentives regularly assessed against intended policy objectives? • Does the evaluation of "benefits" include an assessment of social and environment benefits and positive spillover effects of incentives-motivated investment? • Is the amount of revenue forgone attributable to each tax incentive regularly calculated? • Does the evaluation of "costs" include indirect costs (such as compliance costs, tax administration costs), and revenue leakages due to unintended and unforeseen tax-planning opportunities? • Is a statement on tax expenditures publicly released on a regular basis? • Has the government assessed the largest beneficiaries of tax incentives for investment? Are the largest beneficiaries of tax incentives highlighted in public statements?
Transparency and good governance of tax incentives systems	• What are the legislative provisions governing the tax incentives system? Are they consolidated in the tax law? • Can tax incentives be granted outside of the country's tax and investment laws (e.g. through special agreements, memoranda of understanding, etc.)? • Where taxes could be levied at different levels of government, are the taxing powers and allocation of different tax bases clearly stipulated in the tax laws? • Are tax incentives provided automatically or on a discretionary basis? • For discretionary tax incentives, is the application and qualification process clearly stipulated? Is the process transparent? • Where appropriate, do tax incentives have sunset clauses after which investors are expected to follow the general fiscal rules? • Are all tax incentives for investment consolidated under the authority of one government body? If not, what government entities are mandated to oversee the introduction and granting of tax incentives? • Where different agencies are involved in granting tax incentives, what mechanisms are established to avoid unintended overlap and inconsistencies in application of tax incentives policies? • Where tax incentives are offered subject to eligibility criteria, is monitoring/verification of tax incentive eligibility conditions conducted before and after the qualification?

	• Is the granting and administration of tax incentives decentralised? Can it be carried out by both the central and sub-national governments? • Where tax incentives can be offered at different levels, is the granting and administration of tax incentives coordinated? Is the issue of sub-national tax competition addressed? How?
Countering abusive tax planning strategies domestically and internationally	• Has the government assessed the extent of revenue losses due to domestic and/or cross-border tax planning opportunities? • Has the government critically evaluated the extent to which current/proposed tax incentives interact with the provisions of the country's tax treaties? • Is the government working with their counterparts in other countries to counter abusive cross-border tax planning strategies? • To improve international tax compliance is the country a member of the Global Forum on Transparency and Exchange of Information for Tax Purposes? • Has the government been effective in fighting international tax evasion through participation in a single global standard for automatic exchange of information (AEOI) for tax purposes? • Has the government adopted a co-ordinated international approach and solutions to fighting base erosion and profit shifting (BEPS)?

Additional resources

Altshuler, R. and H. Grubert (2006), "The Role of Governments and MNCs in the Race to the Bottom", *Tax Notes International*, Vol. 41, No. 5, pp. 459-474.

Auerbach, A.J. (1985), "The Theory of Excess Burden and Optimal Taxation", in: Auerbach A.J. and M. Feldstein (eds.), *Handbook of Public Economics*, Vol. 1, North-Holland, Amsterdam, pp. 61-127.

Caiumi, A. (2011), "The Evaluation of the Effectiveness of Tax Expenditures – A Novel Approach: An Application to the Regional Tax Incentives for Business Investments in Italy", *OECD Taxation Working Papers*, No. 5, OECD Publishing, Paris, *http://dx.doi.org/10.1787/5kg3h0 trjmr8-en.*

Devereux, M.P. and R. Griffith (1998), "The Taxation of Discrete Investment Choices", *Institute for Fiscal Studies Working Paper Series*, No. W98/16.

Grubert, H. (2004), "The Tax Burden on Cross-Border Investment: Company Strategies and Country Responses", in: *Measuring the Tax Burden on Labor and Capital*, edited by Birch Sorensen, P., MIT Press (CESifo Seminar Series), Cambridge, Massachusetts, pp. 129-170.

Dirk-Jan Kraan (2004), "Off-budget and Tax Expenditures", *OECD Journal on Budgeting*, Vol. 4/1, *http://dx.doi.org/10.1787/budget-v4-art6-en.*

Johansson, Å. et al. (2008), "Taxation and Economic Growth", *OECD Economics Department Working Papers*, No. 620, OECD Publishing, Paris, *http://dx.doi.org/10.1787/241216205486.*

McKenzie, K.J., M. Mansour and A. Brûlé (1998), "The Calculation of Marginal Effective Tax Rates", *Working Paper*, Vol. 97, No. 5, Technical Committee on Business Taxation, Department of Finance, Canada.

OECD, *The Principles of Transparency and Governance of Tax Incentives for Investment*, Task Force on Tax and Development, OECD, Paris, *www.oecd.org/ctp/tax-global/Transparency_and_Governance_principles.pdf.*

OECD (2011), *Corporate Loss Utilisation through Aggressive Tax Planning*, OECD Publishing, Paris, *http://dx.doi.org/10.1787/9789264119222-en.*

OECD (2011), *Tackling Aggressive Tax Planning through Improved Transparency and Disclosure*, OECD, Paris, *www.oecd.org/ctp/exchangeofinformation/48322860.pdf.*

OECD (2010), *Tax Expenditures in OECD Countries*, OECD Publishing, Paris, *http://dx.doi. org/10.1787/9789264076907-en.*

OECD (2010), *Choosing a Broad Base – Low Rate Approach to Taxation*, OECD Tax Policy Studies, No. 19, OECD Publishing, Paris, *http://dx.doi.org/10.1787/9789264091320-en.*

OECD (2010), *Tax Policy Reform and Economic Growth*, OECD Tax Policy Studies, No. 20, OECD Publishing.

OECD (2009), *Taxation of SMEs: Key Issues and Policy Considerations*, OECD Tax Policy Studies, No. 18, OECD Publishing, Paris, *http://dx.doi.org/10.1787/9789264024748-en.*

OECD (2008), "Tax Effects on Foreign Direct Investment", *Policy Brief*, February, OECD, Paris. *www.oecd. org/daf/inv/investment-policy/40152903.pdf.*

OECD (2007), *Tax Effects on Foreign Direct Investment: Recent Evidence and Policy Analysis*, OECD Tax Policy Studies, No. 17, OECD Publishing, Paris, *http://dx.doi.org/10.1787/9789264038387-en.*

OECD (2007), *Tax Incentives for Investment – A Global Perspective: Experiences in MENA and Non-MENA Countries*, OECD, Paris, *www.oecd.org/mena/investment/38758855.pdf*.

OECD (2005), "Incentives and Free Zones in the MENA Region: A Preliminary Stocktaking", document prepared for Working Group 2 of the MENA-OECD Investment Programme, OECD, Paris, *www.oecd.org/mena/investment/36086747.pdf*.

OECD (2003), *Checklist for Foreign Direct Investment Incentive Policies*, OECD, Paris, *www.oecd.org/daf/inv/investment-policy/2506900.pdf*.

OECD (2003), *Using Micro-Data to Assess Average Tax Rates*, OECD Tax Policy Studies, No. 8, OECD Publishing, Paris, *http://dx.doi.org/10.1787/9789264199811-en*.

OECD (2003), *Tax Policy Assessment and Design in Support of Direct Investment: A Study of Countries in South East Europe*, OECD, Paris, *www.oecd.org/daF/inv/34466352.pdf*.

OECD (2001), *Corporate Tax Incentives for Foreign Direct Investment*, OECD Tax Policy Studies, No. 4, OECD Publishing, Paris, *http://dx.doi.org/10.1787/9789264188402-en*.

OECD (2000), *Tax Burdens: Alternative Measures*, OECD Tax Policy Studies, No. 2, OECD Publishing, Paris, *http://dx.doi.org/10.1787/9789264181588-en*.

Policy Framework for Investment
2015 Edition

6. Corporate governance

As stated in the Preamble to the OECD *Principles of Corporate Governance*, "The degree to which corporations observe basic principles of good corporate governance is an increasingly important factor for investment decisions. Of particular relevance is the relation between corporate governance practices and the increasingly international character of investment. International flows of capital enable companies to access financing from a much larger pool of investors. If countries are to reap the full benefits of the global capital market, and if they are to attract long-term "patient" capital, corporate governance arrangements must be credible, well understood across borders and adhere to internationally accepted principles. Even if corporations do not rely primarily on foreign sources of capital, adherence to good corporate governance practices will help improve the confidence of domestic investors, reduce the cost of capital, underpin the good functioning of financial markets, and ultimately induce more stable sources of financing".

This text and the related questions provide a brief introduction to some of the key corporate governance issues that policy-makers and others should address to promote transparent and efficient markets that support an environment for investment. For a more complete assessment, policy-makers should turn to the OECD *Principles of Corporate Governance* (2004) and the assessment methodology developed by the OECD Corporate Governance Committee (2006), and if possible ask the World Bank for an assessment under the programme of the Reports on Observance of Standards and Codes (ROSC) for Corporate Governance. For countries with significant state ownership of commercially-oriented enterprises, the OECD *Guidelines on Corporate Governance of State-Owned Enterprises* (2005) offer an important complementary set of recommendations.

Both the *Principles of Corporate Governance* and *SOE Guidelines* were in the process of being reviewed at the time that this section was being updated and may feature additional policy and best practice recommendations to be issued later in 2015. However, the core elements of a corporate governance framework that promotes transparent and efficient markets for investment referred to in the text that follows will remain relevant. While this section is based primarily on the recommendations set out in the OECD *Principles* and *SOE Guidelines*, it also draws upon other OECD corporate governance work carried out with both OECD and emerging market economies, including its Regional Corporate Governance Roundtables.

Ensuring an effective corporate governance framework. Effective corporate governance requires an effective legal, regulatory and institutional framework, which all market participants can rely upon when they enter into contractual relations (see also the sections on *Investment Policy* and *Public Governance*). This legal, regulatory and institutional framework typically comprises elements of legislation, regulation, self-regulatory arrangements, voluntary commitments and business practices that are the result of a country's specific economic circumstances, history and traditions. The desirable mix between legislation, regulation, self-regulation, voluntary standards, etc. will therefore vary from country to country.

In this context, designing the regulatory and legal framework that underpins the corporate governance system needs to be flexible enough to meet the needs of corporations operating in widely different circumstances. Another key consideration is the need for effective enforcement and implementation. Among other things, this requires that the allocation of responsibilities for supervision, implementation and enforcement among different authorities be clearly defined so that the competencies of complementary bodies are respected and used most effectively.

Ensuring equitable treatment of shareholders. Equity investors are entitled to certain property rights. For example, an equity share in a publicly traded company can be bought, sold or transferred, and entitles the investor to participate in the company's profits. It also provides a right to obtain information about and influence the company, primarily by voting at shareholder meetings. All these rights carry an intrinsic economic value. In order for investors to buy equity, they therefore need to be confident that their entitlement to these and other rights that they have purchased are properly recognised and protected.

The ownership structure has important implications for the corporate governance framework. In many economies, major shareholders control most companies, in some cases through differential voting rights or complex ownership and control structures that allow them to maintain control with relatively little equity. In other cases, ownership is controlled by the state, raising additional governance challenges. Controlling shareholders have strong incentives to monitor closely the company and its management, but their interests may also conflict with the interests of minority shareholders. Certain conflicts may involve the controlling shareholders extracting private benefits at the expense of minority shareholders.

Companies and their shareholders pay the cost of poor corporate governance through lower valuations, reduced access to equity finance, and difficulties with respect to succession planning and accessing outside talent. Moreover, the economy pays through reduced productivity, as investment funds are allocated less efficiently. To reduce these costs, some controlling shareholders take voluntary measures to improve their own corporate governance and to improve their reputations with other shareholders. Many countries have adopted voluntary measures, such as special stock market tiers and voluntary corporate governance codes, to facilitate the adoption of good practices and to provide companies with a mechanism to signal to markets that they have high standards of corporate governance. While such measures can play an important role in improving corporate governance arrangements, they might leave shareholders and other stakeholders with uncertainty concerning their status and implementation. When codes and principles are used as a national standard or as an explicit substitute for legal or regulatory provisions, market credibility requires that their status in terms of coverage, implementation, compliance and sanctions is clearly specified. In the long run, controlling shareholders may actually benefit from legally binding and effectively enforced measures to improve investor protection.

Addressing conflicts of interest and access to redress. Certain types of corporate activities involve inherent conflicts of interest. It is, therefore, important for the market to know if such activities are carried out with due regard to the interests of all shareholders and to establish effective methods to obtain redress for grievances. The confidence of shareholders and potential investors is enhanced when the legal system provides mechanisms for shareholders to bring lawsuits at a reasonable cost and without excessive delay, but there is some risk that a legal system which enables any investor to challenge corporate activity in the courts can become prone to excessive litigation. A balance must be struck between allowing investors to seek remedies for infringement of ownership rights and avoiding excessive litigation.

An effective judiciary is also essential for providing a credible deterrent to the abuse of shareholder rights. In countries with a weak judiciary, lengthy legal processes with unpredictable outcomes undermine the incentives for shareholders to pursue their rights and discourage potential investors. Another dimension for the redress of violations of shareholder rights is through prevention. It is essential that companies fully disclose material related party transactions to the market, including whether they have been executed at arms-length and on normal market terms. In discussing the content and coverage of such measures, consideration should be given to a workable definition of related parties. It will also be necessary to address the individual's responsibility for announcing a conflict of interest and the role of the board of directors in assessing the material implications of such a conflict.

The role of shareholders. Participation in general shareholder meetings is a fundamental right of all shareholders, both foreign and domestic, and critical to their ability to influence the company. The procedures for notification of shareholder meetings and for casting votes should be designed to facilitate and encourage participation. This requires, inter alia, timely notification and voting systems that enable shareholders to engage in the decision making process at reasonable cost.

Access to information and reliable proxy procedures is a particular challenge in the case of foreign investors who hold their shares through chains of intermediaries. This can give rise to special challenges with respect to determining the entitlement of foreign investors to use their voting rights and the process of communicating with such investors. The obvious risks are that information from the company does not reach the ultimate shareholder and that the opinion of the ultimate shareholder does not reach the shareholder's meeting. It is, therefore, important to address to what extent the legal and regulatory framework clarifies the duties and procedures for informing about the shareholders' meeting, and the procedures for voting of shares that are held by foreign owners.

Ensuring timely, reliable and relevant disclosure. Present and potential shareholders require access to regular, reliable and comparable information in sufficient detail for them to exercise their ownership rights on a fully informed and equal basis. A disclosure regime that promotes transparency is thus a pivotal feature of a market-based corporate governance system. It underpins confidence in the stock market and is a powerful tool for influencing the behaviour of companies and for protecting investor rights. Insufficient or ambiguous information will hamper the ability of the markets to function. It will increase the cost of capital and discourage investment.

A discussion about the content of disclosure standards and the dissemination procedures will naturally address numerous trade-offs that relate to the completeness, quality and cost of establishing and disseminating the information. In order to determine what information should be disclosed at a minimum, many countries apply the concept of materiality. Material information can be defined as information whose omission or misstatement could influence the economic decisions taken by users of information. In the course of developing a strong disclosure regime, the channels, timing and procedures for disseminating corporate information can be just as important as the content of the information itself. Disclosing material information serves a limited purpose if it does not reach the market and the concerned authorities in a cost-effective, easily accessible, predictable and timely fashion.

A particular transparency issue in many markets relates to the complex ownership and control structures. Transparent reporting regarding ownership is essential in order to curb, among other things, abusive transactions among related parties. The OECD template on Options for Obtaining Beneficial Ownership and Control Information serves as a reference for improving the availability of such information.

The central role of the board. The board should play a central role in the governance of the company. The board is chiefly responsible for guiding corporate strategy, for monitoring managerial performance – replacing it if necessary – overseeing systems designed to ensure that the corporation obeys the applicable laws and achieving an adequate return for shareholders. It should also monitor and manage potential conflicts of interest of management, board members and shareholders. In addition, boards have a duty to act in the best interests of the company and its shareholders, and are expected to take due regard of, and deal fairly with, other stakeholder interests, including those of employees, creditors, customers, suppliers and local communities. Corporations should recognise that the contributions of stakeholders constitute a valuable resource for building competitive and profitable companies, contributing to the long-term success of the corporation. The rights of stakeholders as established by law or by mutual agreement should be respected.

Regardless of how the board members are chosen, in order to effectively fulfil their responsibilities, they must be able to exercise informed, objective and independent judgement, acting as representative of all shareholders. Some of their responsibilities are formalised as a duty of care and loyalty, and it is important that these concepts be firmly anchored in law and jurisprudence, and in the understanding and practices of the board members themselves. In some countries, companies have found it useful to articulate explicitly the responsibilities that the board assumes and those for which management is accountable.

The role of voluntary and self-regulatory initiatives. In dealing with corporate governance issues, countries use a varying combination of legal and regulatory instruments, voluntary codes and initiatives, depending in part on history, legal traditions, efficiency of the courts, the political structure of the country and the stage of enterprise development. Many countries, hoping to minimise compliance costs and to provide greater flexibility within a market framework, have developed and sought to promote greater use of voluntary codes and initiatives to improve their corporate governance. In addition, some countries have sought to implement their codes through "comply or explain" provisions that do not require compliance, but require an explanation when the provision is not followed. In some countries, stock exchanges have imposed corporate governance requirements through their listing requirements. The OECD's corporate governance roundtables have seen a rise in the number of countries with corporate governance institutes or institutes of boards of directors to promote awareness and to train directors to understand better corporate governance objectives and requirements. Some institutes have also engaged in media training programmes as another avenue for increasing public understanding of corporate governance.

The importance of country reviews and policy dialogue. This short checklist is not a substitute for a full review of the corporate governance system of a country, and countries should consider undertaking a full review against the OECD *Principles of Corporate Governance*. The World Bank has completed corporate governance reviews of some 50 developing and transition economies, known as Reports on Observance of Standards and Codes (ROSCs), using the OECD Principles as the reference for these exercises. Subject to the agreement of the country's government to have the review publicly disclosed, the World Bank publishes these ROSCs on its web site at *www.worldbank.org/ifa/rosc_cg.html*. In addition, the OECD has developed a methodology providing more detailed guidance for carrying out such reviews. Public discussion and disclosure of these reviews can provide a useful basis for building awareness of and support for changes to strengthen the corporate governance framework and environment for investment. The OECD has also begun recently to carry out more detailed reviews of countries against the OECD's *Guidelines on Corporate Governance of State-Owned Enterprises* (discussed further below), for countries interested in voluntarily adhering to this instrument.

Policy dialogue among policy-makers, institutions and other parties concerned with improving corporate governance has proven to be an effective way of building consensus for corporate governance improvements on a national and regional basis. Corporate governance roundtables (in Asia, the Middle East and North Africa (MENA), Latin America and Russia) continue to meet regularly, and have helped to build consensus for regional and country-based action, and for follow-up on implementation. The OECD has also established regional networks for corporate governance of state-owned enterprises (SOEs) in Asia, MENA, Latin America and Southern Africa. Participation in such regional policy dialogue helps to access international expertise and build capacity – and political will – for change.

Ensuring accountable and well-governed state-owned enterprises. How the ownership function of the state is organised – that is, the functioning of the public sector entities responsible for establishing and implementing the state's ownership policies – can influence the overall investment environment. It is important that the ownership function be clearly identified and separated from other state functions, including regulatory oversight. This helps to ensure a level playing field for all investors, especially with regard to complying with laws and regulations. It also helps to ensure that the state, while being an active and informed owner, does not interfere in the day-to-day management of SOEs, leaving their boards of directors with full operational autonomy to realise their defined objectives, fulfilling their function of strategic guidance and monitoring of management. Board members should be nominated through transparent processes, based on competencies and experience, and it should be clear that their duty is to act in the best interests of the company as a whole. They should not act as individual representatives of the constituencies that appointed them.

Transparency and accountability go hand-in-hand with autonomy. They reassure investors that public sector entities, including SOEs, exercise their powers responsibly and help to instil confidence that investors entering new markets compete on an equal basis. Following some basic corporate governance principles can help SOEs to raise their standards of accountability and transparency. For example, reporting by the SOEs on their performance and achievement of their objectives should be based on the same high-level accounting and auditing standards as for listed companies. This also requires that SOEs develop efficient internal controls and are subject to an annual independent external audit based on internationally recognised standards. Adequate disclosure of material information is also important to foster accountability, in particular relating to any financial assistance received from the state, commitments made on behalf of the state and any material transactions with related entities. Such transactions are often an important source of an uneven playing field for investors, particularly in weak institutional environments. Publishing annually an aggregate report on SOEs, focusing on their objectives, financial and non-financial performance and valuation, also helps to ensure public accountability.

Core questions and principles

Corporate governance framework

1. What steps have been taken to ensure that the corporate governance framework promotes overall economic performance and transparent and well-functioning markets? Has this been translated into a coherent and consistent regulatory framework, backed by effective enforcement?
2. How does the corporate governance framework ensure the equitable treatment of shareholders?
3. What are the institutional structures and mechanisms for legal redress in cases of violation of shareholder rights? Do they function as a credible deterrent to such violations? What measures are in place to monitor and prevent corporate insiders and controlling owners from extracting private benefits?
4. What procedures and institutions are in place to ensure that shareholders have the ability to participate in, and be sufficiently informed on, significant decisions of the company?
5. By what standards and mechanisms do companies meet the market demand for timely, reliable and relevant disclosure, including information about the company's ownership and control structure?
6. How does the corporate governance framework ensure the board plays a central role in the strategic guidance of the company, the effective monitoring of management, and that the board is accountable to the company and its shareholders?
7. Does the framework also recognise the rights of stakeholders established by law or through mutual agreements and encourage active co-operation between corporations and stakeholders in creating wealth, jobs and the sustainability of financially sound enterprises?

Voluntary initiatives

8. What has been done, and what more should be done in terms of voluntary initiatives and training to encourage and develop a good corporate governance culture in the private sector?

Benchmarking

9. Has a review been undertaken of the national corporate governance system against the OECD *Principles of Corporate Governance*? If so, were the results made public?

State-owned enterprises

10. How is the ownership function of state-owned enterprises (SOEs) structured to ensure a separation from the state's regulatory functions, a level playing field vis-à-vis private companies, and clarity of corporate objectives?

11. What are the processes in place to ensure the state does not interfere in day-to-day management of SOEs and that board members act autonomously and effectively carry out their role of strategic oversight?
12. How are SOEs effectively held accountable to the government, parliament, the public, and to non-state shareholders (if any)?

Supplemental questions

Note: The *OECD Principles of Corporate Governance* and *Guidelines on Corporate Governance of State-Owned Enterprises* were under review at the time that this section was being developed, and consensus had not yet been reached on the modifications, so the following questions are based on the previously approved versions of the *Principles* (2004) and *Guidelines* (2005), and should be considered without prejudice to the final outcome of the review of these OECD recommendations. Readers are invited to consult the 2015 version of *Principles* and *Guidelines*. A more complete explanation of criteria to be considered for a corporate governance review may be obtained from the *Methodology for Assessing the Implementation of the OECD Principles of Corporate Governance* (see Additional Resources list).

Corporate governance framework, enforcement and implementation	• What steps have been taken to ensure that the corporate governance framework promotes overall economic performance and transparent and well-functioning markets? • Has this been translated into a coherent and consistent regulatory framework, backed by effective enforcement? • Are rulings timely, transparent and fully explained? Do appeal mechanisms exist? • Do supervisory, regulatory and enforcement authorities have the authority, integrity and resources to fulfil their duties in an effective manner? • Are responsibilities for supervision, implementation and enforcement allocated among different authorities in a clearly defined way so that the competencies of complementary bodies and agencies are respected and used most effectively? • Are potentially overlapping and perhaps contradictory regulations between national jurisdictions monitored so that no regulatory vacuum is allowed to develop (i.e. issues slipping through for which no authority has explicit responsibility)? • What efforts are made to minimise the costs for corporations to comply with multiple legislative systems and to ensure that the costs of compliance are not excessive?
Equitable treatment	• What procedures and institutions are in place to allow shareholders to participate in, and to be sufficiently informed on, significant decisions of the company? • Do they receive timely notification of shareholder meetings? • Do shareholder meetings have voting systems which allow shareholders, including foreign ones, to engage in the decision making process at reasonable cost? • Are proxy procedures reliable and do they enable absent shareholders the possibility to vote for or against resolutions equivalent to shareholders who are present? • What are the procedures and institutional structures for legal redress in cases of violation of shareholder rights? • Do they function as a credible deterrent to such violations? • Does the legal system provide mechanisms for shareholders to bring lawsuits at a reasonable cost and without excessive delay? • How is the balance struck between allowing investors to seek remedies for infringement of ownership rights and avoiding excessive litigation. • Are companies required to disclose fully material related-party transactions to the market and to stipulate whether they have been executed at arm's-length and on normal market terms?
Stakeholders	• Do stakeholders have the opportunity to obtain effective redress for the violation of their rights? • Where stakeholders participate in the governance process, do they have access to relevant, sufficient and reliable information on a timely and regular basis? • Are stakeholders, including individual employees and their representative bodies, freely able to communicate their concerns about illegal or unethical practices to the board without compromising their rights? See also section on *Policies for Enabling Responsible Business Conduct.*

Transparency	• Do disclosure requirements include: ❖ Financial and operating results ❖ Company objectives ❖ Major share ownership and voting rights ❖ Remuneration polices ❖ Qualifications and selection of board members ❖ Related party transactions ❖ Foreseeable risk factors ❖ Issues concerning employee and other stakeholders ❖ Governance structures and policies • Does the corporate governance framework require information to be prepared and disclosed in accordance with high quality, internationally recognised standards of accounting and financial and non-financial disclosure? • Does the framework ensure that annual audits are conducted by an independent, competent and qualified auditor of the company's performance? • What are the channels, timing and procedures for disseminating corporate information? • Does the framework require or encourage information to reach the market in a cost-effective, easily accessible, predictable and timely fashion?
The role of the board of directors	• Are board members' duties of care and loyalty to the company and shareholders firmly anchored in law and jurisprudence and well understood by board members? • To what extent does the corporate governance framework require or encourage boards of directors to perform the following functions: ❖ Reviewing and guiding corporate strategy ❖ Monitoring the effectiveness of the company's governance practices ❖ Monitoring managerial performance ❖ Replacing managers where necessary ❖ Ensuring the integrity of accounting and financial reporting systems and systems of control including for risk management and compliance with the law and relevant standards ❖ Applying high ethical standards including a code of corporate ethics ❖ Monitoring and managing potential conflicts of interest between management, the board and shareholders. • Does the framework require or encourage boards to exercise informed, objective and independent judgement, acting on behalf of all shareholders? • To what extent does the framework require or encourage non-executive board members capable of independent judgement to play a role in cases where there is potential for conflict of interest? • Does the framework encourage or enable boards to play a role in identifying potential members with appropriate knowledge, competencies and expertise through a formal and transparent board nomination process?

Corporate governance of state-owned enterprises

Legal and regulatory framework for SOEs/ ensuring a level playing field	• Are SOEs exempt from the application of general laws, for example with respect to insolvency or bankruptcy procedures, or the treatment of employee remuneration, pension rights and job protection in comparison to private companies? • To what extent has the government enunciated any public service obligations and responsibilities that an SOE is required to undertake beyond those that a private enterprise might have in similar circumstances? By what inter-governmental processes are such requirements developed and specified in laws, regulations or the statutes of the relevant SOEs? • Are the related costs identified, accounted for and disclosed to the general public? • Do stakeholders and competitors have efficient redress if they consider that their rights have been violated? • Do SOEs face competitive conditions regarding access to finance? For instance, are relations with state-owned banks and other SOEs on purely commercial grounds?
The state as owner	• Has the state defined the overall objectives of state ownership and its role in SOE governance? • What government bodies are responsible for defining the ownership policy, and how is it implemented and monitored? • How and by whom are the top corporate executives appointed? If they are appointed by government, what safeguards are in place to ensure their autonomy and accountability to the board of directors? • Are SOE boards granted full responsibility and autonomy to define – in accordance with the objectives defined by the government – strategies for the company? • Is the exercise of ownership rights clearly identified within the state administration? Are these rights centralised or, in case there are several such bodies, how is a sufficient degree of coordination of actions and policies achieved? • Is the ownership or co-ordinating entity held accountable by representative bodies such as parliament? • Does it have clearly defined relationships with relevant bodies, including the state supreme audit?

Equitable treatment of SOE shareholders	• Do the non-state shareholders in SOEs have the same legal rights as shareholders in other companies and as the state? If so, how are these rights enforced? • Do SOEs observe a high degree of transparency towards all shareholders? What mechanisms are in place to ensure that all SOE shareholders have equal and timely access to material information? • Is the participation of minority shareholders in shareholder meetings facilitated? What influence do they have on fundamental corporate decisions such as board elections?
SOE relations with stakeholders	• Are stakeholders' rights established by law and through mutual agreements? If so, how are these rights enforced? • What, if any, formal requirements are there for listed and large SOEs to make public reports on their relations with stakeholders? • Are SOEs required to develop, implement and communicate internal codes of ethics? If so, what compliance programmes are in place, including with regards to measures to prevent fraud and corruption?
SOE disclosure	• What types of financial and non-financial information does the co-ordinating or ownership unit provide on SOEs? Is the information provided in an aggregate form covering all or most SOEs? • Is an internal audit function mandated in SOEs? If so, is it monitored by, and does it report directly to, the board and to the audit committee? • Are SOEs subject to the same accounting and auditing standards as listed companies? • What financial and non-financial information do SOEs disclose? Does the disclosure include the company's objectives and their fulfilment, remuneration of board members and key executives, information on the composition of their boards and their risk management frameworks?
SOE board responsibility	• Insofar as all SOEs have boards of directors, are SOE boards assigned a clear mandate and do they have ultimate responsibility for the company's performance? • Are SOE boards accountable to the owners, the company, or both? Do they ensure that all shareholders are treated equitably? • Do boards have the authority to monitor and, if necessary, replace the CEO? Are the roles of Chair of the board and CEO separated? • Does the composition of SOE boards support their autonomy? In particular, how many independent directors serve in a normal SOE board? • Is employee representation on SOE boards mandated? If so, what, if any, training is provided to employee representatives to prepare them for their board duties? • How common is the use of specialised board committees, such as audit, risk and remuneration committees? • Are SOE boards required to carry out annual evaluations of their performance?

Additional resources

Websites

OECD, *Corporate Affairs*, *www.oecd.org/daf/ca*.

Principles, standards

OECD (2011), *Declaration on International Investment and Multinational Enterprises*, OECD, Paris, *www.oecd.org/investment/investment-policy/oecddeclarationoninternationalinvestmentandmultinationalenterprises.htm*.

OECD (2015), *Guidelines on Corporate Governance of State-Owned Enterprises*, OECD, Paris, *www.oecd.org/daf/ca/oecdguidelinesoncorporategovernanceofstate-ownedenterprises.htm*.

OECD (2015), *Principles of Corporate Governance*, OECD, Paris, *www.oecd.org/daf/ca/oecdprinciplesofcorporategovernance.htm*.

Country reviews and country-specific information

OECD *Corporate Governance Factbook*, OECD, Paris, *www.oecd.org/daf/ca/corporate-governance-factbook.htm*.

OECD (2014), *Risk Management and Corporate Governance*, Corporate Governance, OECD Publishing, Paris, *http://dx.doi.org/10.1787/9789264208636-en*.

OECD (2013), *Supervision and Enforcement in Corporate Governance*, Corporate Governance, OECD Publishing, Paris, *http://dx.doi.org/10.1787/9789264203334-en*.

OECD (2012), *Board Member Nomination and Election*, OECD Publishing, Paris, *http://dx.doi. org/10.1787/9789264179356-en*.

OECD (2012), *Related Party Transactions and Minority Shareholder Rights*, OECD Publishing, Paris, *http://dx.doi.org/10.1787/9789264168008-en*.

OECD (2011), *Board Practices: Incentives and Governing Risks*, Corporate Governance, OECD Publishing, Paris, *http://dx.doi.org/10.1787/9789264113534-en*.

OECD (2011), *The Role of Institutional Investors in Promoting Good Corporate Governance*, Corporate Governance, OECD Publishing, Paris, *http://dx.doi.org/10.1787/9789264128750-en*.

OECD (2010), *State-Owned Enterprise Governance Reform: An Inventory of Recent Change*, OECD, Paris, *www.oecd.org/daf/ca/48455108.pdf*.

OECD (2005), *Corporate Governance of State-Owned Enterprises: A Survey of OECD Countries*, OECD Publishing, Paris, *http://dx.doi.org/10.1787/9789264009431-en*.

OECD (2004), *Corporate Governance: A Survey of OECD Countries*, OECD Publishing, Paris, *http://dx.doi.org/10.1787/9789264106079-en*.

World Bank, Reports on the Observance of Standards and Codes, Corporate Governance, *www.worldbank.org/ifa/rosc_cg.html*.

Other relevant guidance

OECD (2012), *Corporate Governance, Value Creation and Growth: The Bridge between Finance and Enterprise*, Corporate Governance, OECD Publishing, Paris, *http://dx.doi.org/10.1787/9789264179547-en*.

OECD (2010), *Accountability and Transparency: A Guide for State Ownership*, Corporate Governance, OECD Publishing, Paris, *http://dx.doi.org/10.1787/9789264056640-en*.

OECD (2010), *Corporate Governance and the Financial Crisis: Conclusions and Emerging Good Practices to Enhance Implementation of the Principles*, OECD Publishing, Paris, *www.oecd.org/daf/ca/44679170.pdf*.

OECD (2009), *Corporate Governance and the Financial Crisis: Key Findings and Main Messages*, OECD Publishing, Paris, *www.oecd.org/daf/ca/43056196.pdf*.

OECD (2009), *Guide on Fighting Abusive Related Party Transactions in Asia*, OECD Publishing, Paris, *www.oecd.org/daf/ca/43626507.pdf*.

OECD (2009), "Applying RIA to Policy Making in the Area of Corporate Governance", in OECD, *Regulatory Impact Analysis: A Tool for Policy Coherence*, OECD Publishing, Paris, *http://dx.doi.org/10.1787/9789264067110-5-en*.

OECD/IFC (2009), *The Practical Guide to Corporate Governance: Experiences of the Latin American Companies Circle*, *www.oecd.org/daf/ca/43653645.pdf*.

OECD (2007), Methodology for Assessing the Implementation of the OECD Principles of Corporate Governance, OECD Publishing, Paris, *www.oecd.org/daf/ca/37776417.pdf*.

OECD (2002), *Options for Obtaining Beneficial Ownership and Control Information*, OECD Publishing, Paris, *www.oecd.org/corporate/ca/1961539.pdf*.

Policy Framework for Investment
2015 Edition

7. Policies for enabling responsible business conduct

While it is the role of businesses to act responsibly, governments have a duty to protect the public interest and a role in providing an enabling framework for responsible business conduct (RBC). This point goes to the heart of the *Policy Framework for Investment*: to the extent that governments provide an enabling environment for businesses to act responsibly and meet their duty to protect the public interest from potential negative impacts of business activities, they are more likely to keep and attract high quality and responsible investors, minimise the risks of potential adverse impacts of investments, and ensure broader value creation and sustainable development.

Responsible business conduct (RBC) means that businesses a) should make a positive contribution to economic, environmental and social progress with a view to achieving sustainable development and b) should avoid and address adverse impacts through their own activities and prevent or mitigate adverse impacts directly linked to their operations, products or services by a business relationship. Risk-based due diligence is central to identifying, preventing and mitigating actual and potential adverse impacts, and thus is a key element of RBC.

Enterprises must obey domestic laws and respect human rights wherever they operate even where such laws or obligations are poorly enforced. This is the first obligation of enterprises.

The scope of RBC is broad and cross cutting as impacts to society, both positive and negative, cover a range of substantive areas (e.g. disclosure, human rights, employment and labour, environment, anti-corruption, consumer interests, science and technology, competition, and taxation).

All enterprises should behave responsibly regardless of their legal nature, size, ownership structure, or the sector of the economy in which they operate. Thus expectations of RBC extend to enterprises that are private, state-owned, or mixed; multinational or domestic; large or small and medium sized enterprises (SMEs).

Governments can enable RBC in several ways:

- *Regulating* – establishing and enforcing an adequate legal framework that protects the public interest and underpins RBC, and monitoring business performance and compliance with regulatory frameworks;
- *Facilitating* – clearly communicating expectations on what constitutes RBC, providing guidance with respect to specific practices and enabling enterprises to meet those expectations;

- *Co-operating* – working with stakeholders in the business community, worker organisations, civil society, general public, across internal government structures, as well as other governments to create synergies and establish coherence with regard to RBC;
- *Promoting* – demonstrating support for best practices in RBC;
- *Exemplifying* – acting responsibly in the context of the government's role as an economic actor.

Governments enact and enforce the laws and regulations that protect the public interest and underpin RBC

The state duty to protect against human rights infringements is a recognised international human rights obligation, reaffirmed in the *OECD Guidelines for Multinational Enterprises*, the *UN Guiding Principles for Business and Human Rights* and the *ILO Tripartite Declaration on Multinational Enterprises and Social Policy*. This requires taking appropriate steps to prevent, investigate, punish and redress such infringements through effective policies, legislation, regulations and adjudication as well as ensuring that laws and policies concerning investment do not constrain, but rather enable, business to respect human rights. States are encouraged to set clear expectations that businesses respect human rights abroad, as well as at home, particularly with regard to vulnerable individuals and populations.

It is also the duty of governments to ensure that a legal and regulatory framework is in place and enforced in other areas (e.g. employment and labour, environment, anti-corruption, and consumer interests) which can impact the well-being of society. Enforcement requires that governments have sufficient capacity and resources to monitor compliance with laws and regulations and to respond to any infringements.

Governments should facilitate business in meeting RBC expectations and complying with obligations

Governments should provide guidance on appropriate management practices and strive to lower the cost of RBC for business. They should also identify and remove barriers that influence RBC uptake by businesses and should also make an effort to engage with all businesses to strengthen their RBC practices, including with businesses that may have specific challenges with regard to RBC, such as SMEs.

Governments can play a convening role for industry and stakeholders to facilitate collective initiatives to promote RBC among industry and among various stakeholders which can help lower costs and provide broadly supported solutions to issues related to RBC.

Governments can also facilitate and support companies' efforts to comply with regulatory regimes through effective communication with business and relevant stakeholders. This includes communicating expectations regarding RBC as well as establishing channels for dialogue to enable businesses and other stakeholders to seek clarification and advice on expectations relevant to RBC.

Governments should co-operate internally as well as externally with foreign governments and stakeholders to ensure coherence and support of policies relevant to RBC

Governments should ensure coherence among domestic government agencies and bodies to ensure alignment of policies relevant to RBC.

They should also collaborate with foreign governments to establish international policy coherence on RBC in line with widely recognised instruments (e.g. *OECD Guidelines for Multinational Enterprises*, the *UN Guiding Principles for Business and Human Rights*) which contribute to a global level-playing field for investment.

RBC has broad-reaching impacts and therefore the process of defining expectations of RBC and implementing those expectations requires consultation and co-operation amongst all relevant stakeholders – including among government agencies, companies, worker associations, professional associations, employer associations, civil society, and local communities. Governments should consult with companies and other stakeholders on existing or potential RBC policies or enforcement practices. Government should also create an enabling environment for stakeholders to engage in monitoring and promotion of RBC.

Governments should recognise and support RBC which makes a positive contribution to economic, environmental or social progress

Both government and non-government standards and instruments can contribute to RBC. In addition to enacting and enforcing regulation that protects the public interest and underpins RBC, governments can encourage or contribute to non-government initiatives related to RBC.

They should provide recognition and incentives to businesses that exemplify best practices with regard to RBC to encourage strong RBC performance. For example, governments can encourage specific public interest goals through tax benefits that encourage businesses to make a positive contribution to economic, environmental or social progress. Governments can also promote RBC through their own economic activities, by engaging with enterprises recognised for behaving responsibly, beyond simply meeting their legal obligations (e.g. through certification, participation in voluntary initiatives etc.). For example, this can be done through inclusion of public procurement criteria or public financing terms related to RBC, but care should be taken to ensure that such actions are not used for protectionist purposes. Governments can also recognise best practices through an annual awards programme.

Governments should exemplify RBC in their own role within the economy

Governments often act as economic actors (e.g. through their role as employers, procurers and through state-owned enterprises) and are expected to behave responsibly when performing a commercial role. By exemplifying RBC through its own operations the government enhances its legitimacy in making recommendations on RBC to business.

Core questions and principles

1. Does the government establish and enforce an adequate legal and regulatory framework that protects the public interest and underpins RBC?
2. Does the government promote RBC among domestic companies operating abroad?
3. Does the government facilitate enterprises' ability to meet expectations of RBC?
4. Does the government effectively communicate what constitutes RBC to companies and other stakeholders?
5. Does the government work towards ensuring internal policy coherence and alignment with regard to RBC standards and guidance?

6. Does the government co-operate with other governments in promoting international policies and principles for RBC?
7. Does the government support stakeholder involvement in RBC?
8. Does the government provide support and incentives to companies to strengthen RBC?
9. Does the government behave responsibly in the context of its role within the economy (e.g. as an employer, investor, or through state-owned enterprises)?
10. Does the government promote transparency around RBC, including through non-financial disclosure and reporting requirements?

Supplemental questions

Establishing and enforcing a legal and regulatory framework	• Has the government ratified the main international human rights, labour, environmental and anti-bribery conventions and incorporated them into domestic law? • Does the domestic legal regulatory framework align with internationally recognised instruments on RBC (e.g. OECD Guidelines for Multinational Enterprises, the UN Guiding Principles for Business and Human Rights, ILO Core Conventions)? • Does the government implement and enforce laws and regulations which protect the public interest from the potential negative impacts of business activities and underpin RBC? • Does the government provide human and financial resources to relevant government agencies to ensure development and enforcement of an adequate legal and regulatory framework to underpin RBC? • Does the government provide effective, secure, adequately funded and publically accessible legal processes for investors and for persons that are adversely impacted by the actions of an enterprise? • Does the government allow for non-judicial mechanisms for conflict resolution involving investors and persons that are adversely impacted by the actions of an enterprise, for example through mediation and conciliation? Further questions relating to core labour standards, financial accountability and the environment can be found in the sections on *Developing Human Resources for Investment, Corporate Governance* and *Investment Framework for Green Growth.*
Encouraging RBC throughout international operations	• Does the government encourage domestic companies operating abroad to respect international RBC instruments including the OECD Guidelines for Multinational Enterprise and the UN Guiding Principles for Human Rights and Business? • Does the government encourage domestic companies operating abroad to conduct due diligence across business relationships, including throughout supply chains, to address actual and potential adverse social and environmental impacts? • Does the government facilitate companies in reporting suspected violations of international law, or risks of violations, related to their business operations? (e.g. as outlined in the Voluntary Principles on Human Rights and Security or in UN Sanctions).
Facilitating enterprises in meeting expectations of RBC	• How does the government communicate as to what constitutes RBC and provide advice and guidance to companies on how to meet these expectations? • Does the government offer guidance or capacity-building on appropriate management practices to meet these expectations? • Does the government engage in efforts to remove barriers and lower the costs of RBC? • Does the government take specific actions to involve and encourage SMEs and other companies that may lag behind to respect RBC principles and standards?
Communicating on RBC expectations	• Does the government have a national RBC policy or action plan to promote RBC? • Has the government appointed a special dedicated body or representative within government responsible for coordinating RBC activities and promotion? • Does the government communicate expectations on RBC through other relevant bodies such as investment promotion agencies, public relations bodies etc.? • Does the government provide clear and accessible information on responsible business practices to stakeholders? • Does the government provide channels for dialogue to help businesses and other stakeholders obtain clarification and advice on expectations of RBC?
Establishing policy coherence and alignment on RBC	• Does the government ensure coordination across relevant domestic government bodies as well as with sub-national government bodies and authorities on cross cutting issues related to RBC? • Does the government incorporate RBC considerations into sectoral master plans and/or other private sector development strategies? • Does the government include references to expectations on RBC in international economic instruments (e.g. trade and investment policy, export credit agreements, official development assistance)?

Promoting international RBC policies and principles	• Does the government engage in international dialogue on RBC? • How does the government encourage broad participation, including by developing countries, in international, regional and bilateral initiatives on RBC, for example through donor agencies, diplomatic action, etc.? • Has the government adhered to or participated in, or does it consider doing so, any of the following: ❖ OECD Guidelines for Multinational Enterprises? ❖ UN Guiding Principles on Business and Human Rights? ❖ ILO Tripartite Declaration of Principles concerning Multinational Enterprises and Social Policies?
Supporting stakeholder involvement in RBC	• Does the government engage actively with stakeholders (e.g. industry, civil society, worker organisations, local communities) on enabling RBC? What mechanisms for engagement exist? • Are consultations with stakeholders held on existing and proposed laws and regulations on a local, regional and national basis (see section on *Horizontal policies and practices*)? • Are the rights of "whistle-blowers", individuals or organisations who draw attention to legal misconduct (e.g. with regards to human rights, environmental or social regulations) of either government or business, explicitly protected by the law? • Are individuals and organisations able to research and publish information on human rights, environmental concerns and related issues without fear of reprisal or punishment? • Are civil society organisations supported and encouraged in taking part in international and multi-stakeholder RBC initiatives?
Providing support and incentives for strengthened RBC	• Does the government provide financial incentives to encourage businesses to make a positive contribution to economic, environmental or social progress (e.g. credits to companies for demonstrated commitment to RBC in government contracting, procurement processes, investment; through tax incentives)? • Does it provide other incentives, such as annual RBC awards of recognition to companies for acting responsibly, beyond simply meeting their legal obligations? • Does it have criteria in place to avoid protectionism when using contracting and procurement processes and/or providing other financial incentives to promote strengthened RBC among companies? • Does it use its convening power to help support collective initiatives related to RBC? • Does it support widely-recognised, non-government measures and initiatives relevant to RBC (e.g. multi-stakeholder initiatives, industry standards, bottom-up mechanisms or standards negotiated with stakeholders at local level)?
Exemplifying RBC	• Does the government model high RBC standards and principles in its own practices, e.g. as an employer, business partner, commercial enterprise? • Does the government, through its public contracting and procurement processes, promote high standards of transparency and objectivity? • Do state-owned enterprises model best practices in terms of RBC, including through disclosure of non-financial information and reporting related to environmental and social governance practices?
Promoting transparency around RBC	• What standards for corporate reporting does the government promote, including financial, environmental and social governance reporting, in line with international guidelines (e.g. Global Reporting Initiative)? • Does the government mandate disclosure of information on non-financial performance for companies seeking support from bodies managing public funds such as Export Credit Agencies? • Does the government encourage reporting by domestic companies operating abroad on areas relevant to RBC (e.g. the respect of human rights throughout supply chain)?

Additional resources

Websites

OECD Guidelines for Multinational Enterprises, *http://mneguidelines.oecd.org/.*

International organisations:

International Labour Organization: *www.ilo.org*

Organisation for Economic Co-operation and Development (OECD) *www.oecd.org*

United Nations: *www.unodc.org; www.unepfi.org; www.unfccc.int*

OECD Institutional Stakeholders:

Business and Industry Advisory Committee to the OECD (BIAC), *http://biac.org/*

Trade Union Advisory Committee to the OECD (TUAC), *www.tuac.org/*

OECD Watch, *http://oecdwatch.org/*

Non-profit organisations:

Amnesty International: *www.amnesty.org*.

Business and Human Rights Resource Centre: *www.business-humanrights.org*.

CDP: *www.cdproject.net*.

Global Reporting Initiative (GRI): *www.globalreporting.org*.

Human Rights Watch: *www.hrw.org*.

International Business Leaders' Forum: *www.iblf.org*.

International Trade Union Confederation: *www.ituc-csi.org/*.

Transparency International: *www.transparency.org*.

World Business Council for Sustainable Development: *www.wbcsd.org; www.ihrb.org*.

World Wildlife Fund: *www.wwf.org*.

Authoritative principles and standards

ILO Tripartite Declaration of Principles concerning Multinational Enterprises and Social Policy (2014), International Labour Organisation, *www.ilo.org/empent/Publications/WCMS_094386/lang--en/index.htm*.

ILO Declaration on Fundamental Principles and Rights at Work (1998), International Labour Organisation *www.ilo.org/declaration/lang--en/index.htm*.

OECD (2015), *OECD Guidelines on Corporate Governance of State-Owned Enterprises*, OECD, Paris, *www.oecd.org/corporate/ca/oecdguidelinesoncorporategovernanceofstate-ownedenterprises.htm*.

OECD (2015), *OECD Principles of Corporate Governance*, OECD, Paris, *www.oecd.org/corporate/oecdprinciplesofcorporategovernance.htm*.

OECD (2012), *OECD Recommendation on Common Approaches for Officially Supported Export Credits and Environmental and Social Due Diligence*, *www.oecd.org/tad/xcred/oecd-recommendations.htm*.

OECD (2011), *OECD Guidelines for Multinational Enterprises*, OECD Publishing, Paris, *http://dx.doi.org/10.1787/9789264115415-en*.

OECD (2006), *OECD Recommendation on Bribery and Officially Supported Export Credit*, OECD, Paris, *www.oecd.org/tad/xcred/anti-briberymeasures.htm*.

OECD (1997), *OECD Convention on Combatting Bribery of Foreign Public Officials in International Business Transactions*, OECD, Paris, *www.oecd.org/corruption/oecdantibriberyconvention.htm*.

UN Guiding Principles on Business and Human Rights, United Nations, *www.ohchr.org/Documents/Publications/GuidingPrinciplesBusinessHR_EN.pdf*.

UN Universal Declaration of Human Rights, United Nations.

UN Principles for Responsible Investment, United Nations, *www.unpri.org*.

Other standards and initiatives

Ethical Trade Initiative, *www.ethicaltrade.org*.

Extractive Industries Transparency Initiative, *https://eiti.org/*.

Fair Labour Association, *www.fairlabor.org*.

ISO 14000 – Environmental management, *www.iso.org/iso/home/standards/management-standards/iso14000.htm*.

ISO 26000 – Social responsibility, *www.iso.org/iso/home/standards/iso26000.htm*.

Kimberley Process, *www.kimberleyprocess.com*.

Open Contracting Principles, *www.open-contracting.org/global_principles*.

UN Global Compact, *www.unglobalcompact.org/*.

UN-CFS Voluntary Guidelines on the Governance of Tenure, Forestry and Fisheries in the context of National Food Security, *www.fao.org/nr/tenure/voluntary-guidelines/en/*.

UN-CFS Responsible Agricultural Investment Principles in the Context of National Food Security, *www.fao.org/cfs/cfs-home/resaginv/en/*.

Voluntary Principles on Security and Human Rights, *www.voluntaryprinciples.org/*.

Tools, guidance, manuals

BIAC Anti-Bribery Resource Guide, *www.member.biac.org/pubs/anti-bribery_resource/guide.htm*.

Business Anti-Corruption Portal, *www.business-anti-corruption.com/*.

Fox, T., H. Ward and B. Howard (2002), *Public Sector Roles in Strengthening Corporate Social Responsibility: A Baseline Study*, Corporate Responsibility for Environment and Development Programme, International Institute for Environment and Development (IIED), World Bank, Washington, DC.

OECD, *Risk Awareness Tool for Multinational Enterprises in Weak Governance Zones*, *www.oecd.org/investment/mne/weakgovernancezones-riskawarenesstoolformultinational enterprises-oecd.htm*.

OECD, *Due Diligence for Responsible Supply Chains of Minerals from Conflict-Affected and High-Risk Areas*, *www.oecd.org/corporate/mne/mining.htm*.

OECD, *Watch Guide to the OECD Guidelines*, *http://oecdwatch.org/publications-en/Publication_1664*.

Open Government Resource Materials, *www.opengovpartnership.org/*.

Trade Union Guide to the OECD Guidelines for Multinational Enterprises, *www.tuacoecdmneguidelines.org/Docs/TradeUnionGuide.pdf*.

Reviews, case/country studies

United Nations, *Protect, Respect and Remedy: A Framework for Business and Human Rights*, Report of the Special Representative of the Secretary-General on the issue of human rights and transnational corporations and other business enterprises, John Ruggie.

OECD (2005), *Corporate Governance of State-Owned Enterprises: A Survey of OECD Countries*, OECD Publishing, Paris, *http://dx.doi.org/10.1787/9789264009431-en*.

OECD (2001), *Corporate Responsibility: Private Initiatives and Public Goals*, OECD Publishing, Paris, *http://dx.doi.org/10.1787/9789264193062-en*.

Indicators

ILOLEX database on international labour standards, *www.ilo.org/ilolex/english/*.

NATLEX database on labour, social security and related human rights legislation, *www.ilo.org/dyn/natlex/*.

ECOLEX information service on environmental law, *www.ecolex.org/*.

World Bank Governance Indicators, *www.govindicators.org/*.

Transparency International Corruption Perceptions Index, *www.transparency.org/research/cpi/overview*.

UN Sustainable Development Goals, *https://sustainabledevelopment.un.org/*.

UN Office of the High Commission for Human Rights database on countries' ratification of human rights conventions, *www.ohchr.org/EN/HRBodies/Pages/TreatyBodies.aspx*.

Policy Framework for Investment
2015 Edition

8. Developing human resources for investment

Competitively skilled and flexible human resources are at the centre of a country's competitiveness to attract investment and sustain economic growth, as companies constantly restructure their global supply chains. Human resource development (HRD) thus features prominently among the various policies affecting a country's enabling environment for investment and economic development.

Human resource development is the process of increasing the knowledge, skills, and capacities of all people in a society.* HRD policies concern the quality of the labour force and the regulation of the labour market. Governments can take policy action to improve human resources directly, such as through education and health policies, but they can also put in place policies to help and encourage companies to invest in human resources, for example through on-the-job training, and employer involvement in education. Well-designed labour policies can help reduce inequality and spur economic growth, create more and better jobs for all, allow investment in worker skills, and enhance access to, and improve the quality of, education, training and overall public services. Effective HRD policies cannot be shaped in isolation and should be a part of a coherent and comprehensive framework in line with the country's development and investment strategies. Direct dialogue with workers and workers' organisations is the best means of determining workers' needs in terms of wages, working conditions and skills development.

Even more important than these individual HRD policies is the interaction among them. Attempts to boost workforce skills through vocational training without considering their interaction with basic educational attainment or flanking labour market policies are likely to be ineffective. Human resource development requires a comprehensive strategy that takes full account of the linkages between, for example, improved population health on educational attainment and, depending on employment policies, on labour productivity.

The quality and adaptability of the labour force are key drivers in creating a favourable environment for both domestic and foreign enterprises to grow through new investment and to adapt quickly to changing circumstances. Quality is largely determined by education, training programmes and the overall health of the population. Adaptability refers to the capacity of the labour force and education systems to adjust to new challenges, including economic diversification and upgrading in global value chains, as is highlighted in the sections on *Trade policy* and *Investment promotion and facilitation*.

* Harbison, Frederick and Myers, Charles A. (1964) *Education, Manpower and Economic Growth: Strategies of Human Resources Development*, McGraw-Hill, USA, p. 2.

In a global economy increasingly dependent on skills, countries with lower skill levels need to ensure they develop their human capital in order to boost their competitiveness. Broad access to quality primary education and early childhood education and care is a core requirement in developing a skilled workforce and provides foundations for future learning. Secondary and tertiary education as well as vocational education and training, including on relevant skills for an individual's full and effective participation in the labour market, help reap the full benefits of investment by increasing local value-addition. Public health and access to healthcare also affect human resources and the attractiveness of the business environment, as good health improves worker productivity. Also, effective strategies to attract workers with different sets of skills can address skill needs, facilitate knowledge transfer, and promote competitiveness while mitigating potential negative effects on the domestic labour force. Skills strategies should further consider and make the most of all available human capital, including attracting the return of highly-skilled individuals who have studied abroad and engaging with diaspora communities to promote skills, knowledge and innovation opportunities.

Training programmes for individuals entering and working in companies can complement formal education by developing business skills and firm-specific knowledge which are key to unlocking an individual's productive potential and enabling career mobility. Internships and co-operative programmes with educational institutions are proven strategies, and businesses should also be encouraged to help develop the skills of their employees through, for example, on-the-job training or by funding specialised education to benefit both the company and the employee. Training programmes can increase productivity and the spill-overs from MNEs to local firms with higher absorptive capacity for new knowledge and technology – an aspect that is further explained in the section on *Investment promotion and facilitation*. With all forms of education and training, policy action can help ensure that programmes are of good quality and accessible, meet business needs and are regularly reviewed. Policy can further promote integrated and ongoing links between education and training institutions and providers, businesses and industry to tailor educational programmes to business needs and to provide young people with the information needed to make realistic choices about their studies for future employment. Effective HRD and training practices are equally important in public institutions to increase the capacity of the public sector.

Labour standards are essential to ensure that business contributes to local social and economic development. Core labour standards are fundamental principles protecting basic human rights in the workforce and can enhance inclusive private sector-led growth. The International Labour Organisation (ILO) has identified eight internationally agreed conventions as fundamental, a majority of which have been ratified by most countries. As stated in the ILO *Declaration on Fundamental Principles and Rights at Work* (1998) the core labour standards aim to: 1) eliminate all forms of forced or compulsory labour; 2) effectively abolish child labour; 3) eliminate discrimination in respect of employment and occupation; and 4) ensure the freedom of association and the right to collective bargaining. The OECD *Guidelines for Multinational Enterprises* echo relevant provisions of the 1998 *Declaration*, as well as the 1977 ILO *Tripartite Declaration of Principles concerning Multinational Enterprises and Social Policy*, last revised in 2006. The *Guidelines*, as a non-binding instrument, promote observance of these standards and principles. Enforcement of core labour standards also benefits the whole economy by creating a level playing field for foreign and domestic investors and by improving economic performance. The elements addressed in this section complement the discussion of the section on *Policies for enabling responsible business conduct.*

Labour market regulation must both reach the social goals of employment protection – the protection of core labour standards, occupational health and safety standards, minimum wage regulation, restrictions on hiring and firing, and legal guarantees of social insurance regimes – and address the need to enable companies to invest and create jobs, and in doing so contribute to boosting productivity and economic growth through the appropriate government-created frameworks. Labour market regulations that focus too much on protecting and improving the income and benefits of existing workers can dissuade job creation and discourage investment, or even create incentives for employers and workers alike to shift to, or remain in, the informal economy, where workers are not protected by labour laws and lack access to work-related measures of social protection. The informal economy is estimated to comprise a major part of non-agricultural employment in developing countries. Specific strategies are needed to encourage workers to move into the formal economy and to address social protection for workers in the informal sectors, including those SMEs that are unable to afford private insurance against risk. In the formal economy, the co-operation and involvement of private enterprises in maintaining high standards and protecting workers, and a willingness on their part to negotiate in good faith with legitimate workers' organisations, are needed to achieve the best policy outcomes.

Beyond labour standards, an efficient labour market requires that all those who are capable of contributing to the economic and social development of a country are in a position to do so. This means that explicit or implicit discrimination, including on the grounds of race, sex or age, must be prevented. It requires an appropriate legislative framework, but also effective implementation and enforcement of relevant educational, social and labour market policies and active monitoring of relevant outcomes. The OECD *Gender Recommendation* (2013) provides a framework for assessing the relevant legislative approach to be followed. Individuals and groups may also become excluded from the labour market due to their lack of skills, family circumstances, health and long-term joblessness. Appropriate incentives and the use of active labour market policies, such as job-search assistance and training, can help minimise such exclusion, and increase the stock of skills available in the labour market.

As new technologies and shifting market structures are constantly changing the needs of businesses, the flexibility and adaptability of the overall HRD framework are fundamental to the competitiveness of economies. To guarantee this, policy makers need to co-operate closely with the main stakeholders and undertake periodic assessments of the impact of policies on the business and investment environments. A general challenge of governments is to develop HRD policies that encourage the engagement of individual companies to adhere to good HRD practices. This includes ensuring their operations comply with international principles and standards including those provided in the OECD *Guidelines for Multinational Enterprises* and contributing effectively to the development of appropriate frameworks to support and enable compliance.

Core questions and principles

1. Has the government established a coherent and comprehensive human resource development (HRD) policy framework consistent with its broader development and investment strategy and its implementation capacity?

2. Is there an effective system for tackling discrimination that affects labour market outcomes?
3. What steps has the government taken to increase participation in basic schooling and to improve the quality of instruction so as to leverage human resource assets to attract and to seize investment opportunities?
4. Is the economic incentive sufficient to encourage individuals to invest in higher education and life-long learning, supporting improvements in the investment environment through a more qualified human resource base?
5. To what extent does the government promote effective training programmes, including through involving the private sector?
6. Does the government have an affordable, effective and efficient overall health system?
7. What mechanisms are being put in place to promote and enforce core labour standards?
8. To what extent do labour market regulations support job creation and the government's investment attraction strategy?
9. How does the government assist large-scale labour adjustments? What role is business encouraged to play in easing the transition costs associated with labour adjustment?
10. What steps are being taken to ensure that labour market regulations support an adaptable workforce and maintain the ability of enterprises to modify their operations and investment planning?
11. To what extent does the government allow companies to recruit workers from abroad when they are unable to obtain the skills needed from the domestic labour market?

Supplemental questions

Overall HRD framework for investment and development	• How is the effectiveness and consistency of the HRD policy framework ensured vis-à-vis the overall investment and development strategy? • Is the HRD policy framework periodically reviewed to ensure that it is responsive to new economic developments? • How are the main stakeholders, including the private sector, identified and engaged in developing the HRD framework? • How does the government ensure access to basic education, a human right and a minimum necessary condition for development, for girls and boys? • What efforts are underway to strengthen the quality of formal education, which provides the foundations for further learning and safeguards the capacity to seize future investment opportunities? • How does policy combat gender discrimination in remuneration and career progression? What initiatives have been introduced to increase the presence of women on boards and in senior and middle management positions? • What policies (such as childcare, child-related leave, and out-of-school hours care) are in place to support parents in work? • Are benefits and social support financed and distributed in such a way as to avoid discrimination, intended or otherwise, between men and women or different social groups?
Enhancing skills and entrepreneurship inclusively	• How does the government measure and assess the skills level in the economy? • Does the current system of higher education provide the incentives for skilled workers to stay in the country, thus contributing to a more competitive and skilled labour force? • How does the government evaluate the returns from its higher education programmes for graduates? • What measures are taken to track, address and avoid the mismatch between supply and demand for labour in the economy? Is labour market analysis backed by the adaptation of skills development for employment and job placement systems? • How is investment of scarce resources in skills prioritised? Does the government consider ways of combining public and private resources to fund skills development, as well as designing effective incentives for individuals and employers? • How does the government channel the skills demand from industry into its skills enhancement strategy? (See section on investment promotion and facilitation) • Does the government have a well-functioning vocational and technical training system that provides the economy with the necessary skills? Does the current system adequately promote entrepreneurship and training for self-employment, business or civil society start-ups, business skills and financial literacy, including for the youth?

- How does the government evaluate the effectiveness and impact of its training measures and programmes and review and adjust these accordingly? Are measures to ensure training quality and accreditation adequate?
- Is funding for skills development adequate and sustainable?
- How does the government strengthen the knowledge triangle between the government, institutions of higher education and higher education stakeholders in its economy? (See section *Investment promotion and facilitation*)
- Does the private sector contribute to the development of the curricula in the system?
- What mechanisms are used to encourage businesses to offer training to employees and to play a larger role in co-financing training?
- Are on-the-job training measures promoted, including through apprenticeships for the youth?
- How does the government promote gender equality in access to education and training?
- What measures exist to enhance the inclusiveness and gender equality in the access to the study of science, technology, engineering, mathematics (STEM), financial and entrepreneurship issues, as well as arts and the humanities?

Health and occupational safety

- Has the government established coherent procedures to evaluate public health expenditures aimed at improving public health outcomes and, through inter-linkages, the investment environment?
- How does the government tackle chronic diseases and the unhealthy lifestyles associated with them?
  - What measures are in place to prevent and control the spreading of infectious diseases?
  - How does the government ensure that occupational health and safety system standards are upheld and implemented, including by small and medium-size enterprises?
  - What measures are in place to protect workers from adverse effects from chemicals, pesticides, biotechnology & nanomaterials?
- Is there an effective strategy to promote good mental health?

Core labour standards

- Has the government signed and ratified the fundamental ILO conventions related to core labour standards? Does the government comply with these conventions in practice, regardless of whether they have been ratified? What measures are in place to ensure and promote the effective implementation of these conventions?
- What measures has the government taken to:
  - eliminate all forms of forced or compulsory labour and abolish child labour;
  - uphold the principles of non-discrimination with respect to employment and occupation;
  - ensure the freedom of association and the right to collective bargaining?
- What action has the government taken to ensure public awareness of the laws and regulations to defend the core labour standards?
- Does existing outreach communicate the necessary information in a manner that is clear and complete yet user-friendly, and which reaches its intended audience, i.e. workers, employers, potential local and foreign investors and organisations representing each of these groups?
- How are the actions of non-governmental actors, including workers' and employers' organisations, to promote the implementation of core labour standards, either in conjunction with, or independent of, the government, strengthened and promoted? Are there tripartite consultation bodies at national, provincial and local levels to provide workers' and employers' organisations a forum to discuss and influence labour policies?
- How does the government ensure nation-wide implementation of these standards, including in special economic and export processing zones and to cover foreign workers?

See the section on *Policies for Enabling Responsible Business Conduct* for more questions on international labour standards

Labour market regulation for business

- How does the government ensure an adequate employment protection framework, while allowing sufficient flexibility to enhance productivity and overall competitiveness in the economy?
- What initiatives have been introduced that support policy coordination, balancing social objectives, the goal of a competitive workforce and the incentives for business to invest?
- What measures exist to limit working hours? Does legislation impede flexible working time arrangements?
- What restrictions exist on hiring and firing, such as the types of work contracts (fixed-term, open-ended, and part-time) and legal restrictions on firing?
- What measures are in place to protect workers at the margin of the labour force, including in the informal sector and migrant workers, if owing to their situation they are not covered by labour laws or social protection schemes?
- Does policy have a discouraging effect on employment in the formal sector? Do taxes and social security contributions excessively penalise those in the formal sector relative to the informal? Do regulations discourage operating in the formal economy?
- How does the legal framework in place contribute to fighting discrimination in the workplace?
- What are the administrative and financial burdens associated with the employment of foreign workers?

Supporting labour adjustments

- What retraining and redeployment programmes are in effect and how well do they operate?
  - Are the programmes government-run, operated privately or a hybrid? Does the corresponding government agency provide a valuable service not already available elsewhere?
  - How easily accessible are the programmes? Do people know about and actually use the services provided?
  - What role do the business community and labour organisations play in ensuring the programmes are responsive to their needs, for example, by advising on the types of training most in demand or providing information on job availability?

	• What types of financial assistance are mandated through labour and social security laws and regulations? Do the laws and regulations: ❖ Provide a meaningful cushion to those negatively affected by labour adjustments? ❖ Balance interests of business and labour by providing protection that is both effective and not overly burdensome? ❖ Are the laws and regulations effectively enforced? • What role do businesses play in facilitating the transition process in labour adjustments? How do businesses co-operate with both labour and government? What mechanisms encourage businesses to: ❖ Communicate regularly with labour to keep employees informed of the state of company affairs; ❖ Consult labour early on to address financial difficulties that may result in layoffs; ❖ Keep government entities abreast of projected large-scale firings so the government can mobilise to provide needed assistance? • Are there any mandatory notice requirements for layoffs of a certain size and does this approach effectively meet the goal of assisting labour while not excessively burdening management, since overregulation can discourage investment?
Labour mobility and migration	• Do internal or cross-border migrant workers in the country enjoy the same level of protection of their fundamental rights as local workers? • Are migration policies aligned with the need to address skills shortages in the economy? • Are safeguards to protect the domestic labour market and promote skill development locally proportionate and fairly applied? • Do laws and regulations allow the deployment of foreign workers from an enterprise investing in the host country? If there are restrictions, are they transparent and related to safeguarding the local labour market? • Do personnel deployed by investing enterprises benefit from speedy visa issuance or other favourable conditions? What steps have been taken to unwind unduly restrictive practices? (See the section on *Investment Policy*) • Are workers with needed skills allowed or encouraged to migrate to the country for work purposes? • What measures exist to maximise the full benefit of a country's investment in its own human resources, including attracting nationals who have completed their studies abroad?
Flexibility and efficiency of labour market regulations	• How does the government ensure and maintain flexibility and efficiency of its labour laws and regulations? • Are these laws and regulations made with appropriate consultation with employers and workers' organisations? • How efficient and easily intelligible are the economic dismissal laws and regulations? • Must employers consult or obtain prior approval from government or other bodies (e.g. labour inspectors, courts, union representatives)? Are employers required to respect certain priority rules for dismissal? • How many steps are involved in laying off employees for economic reasons and can any be removed? • What is the likelihood of ending up in court over a dispute? • Regarding flexicurity protections, has the country, within its means, successfully implemented laws, regulations and other programmes that provide income support and redeployment services to the unemployed, while reducing legislative and regulatory barriers to personnel restructuring? • What types of support measures exist (e.g. direct financial support to the unemployed or other forms of unemployment insurance, severance pay from employers)? • Regarding flexible work schedules, what laws and regulations govern work schedules, including work-hour limitations and fixed-term and part-time work contracts? Do tax and social security regulations discriminate against part-time work or flexible work arrangements? • What measures are in place to ensure that the interests of any relevant stakeholders are not neglected or under-represented through the current laws and regulations?

Additional resources

Websites

OECD, *Skills Strategy*, *www.oecd.org/edu/oecdskillsstrategy.htm*.

OECD, *Higher Education Programme*, *www.oecd.org/edu/imhe*.

OECD, Programme for International Student Assessment, *www.oecd.org/pisa*.

OECD, Skills Surveys, Programme for the International Assessment of Adult Competencies (PIAAC), *www.oecd.org/site/piaac*.

OECD, *Gender Equality*, *www.oecd.org/gender*.

OECD, *Identify and mobilise migrants' skills for development*, *www.oecd.org/migration/diasporas.htm*.

Tools, guidance, manuals

Brezzi, M. and M. Piacentini (2010), "*Labour Mobility and Development Dynamics in OECD Regions*".

OECD (2013), *Recommendation of the Council on Gender Equality in Education, Employment and Entrepreneurship*, OECD, Paris, *www.oecd.org/gender/C-MIN%282013%295-ENG.pdf*.

OECD (2012), *Free Movement of Workers and Labour Market Adjustment: Recent Experiences from OECD Countries and the European Union*, OECD Publishing, Paris, *http://dx.doi.org/10.1787/9789264177185-en*.

OECD/European Union (2012), *Policy brief on youth entrepreneurship*, Publications Office of the European Union, Luxembourg, *www.oecd.org/employment/leed/Youth%20entrepreneurship%20policy%20brief%20EN_FINAL.pdf*.

OECD/French Ministry of Foreign Affairs (2012), *Harnessing the skills of migrants and diaspora to foster development: policy options*, French Ministry of Foreign Affairs, Paris, *www.oecd.org/migration/Policy_Brief_Migrants_En_BD%20DEFINITIF.pdf*.

Stone, S., P. Sourdin and C. Legendre (2013), "Trade and Labour Market Adjustment", *OECD Trade Policy Papers*, No. 143, OECD Publishing, Paris, *http://dx.doi.org/10.1787/5k4c6spvddwj-en*.

Policy Framework for Investment
2015 Edition

9. Investment in infrastructure

A crucial input to growth and connectivity. Poor quality or inadequate economic infrastructure – electricity, water and sanitation, communication and transport network systems – raises costs for all firms and restricts the flow of goods, services, people and market information both within the economy and abroad, with implications for countries' integration into global value chains and broader economic development. By segregating markets, infrastructure weaknesses limit competition, thus dulling incentives to innovate and to improve productivity. All firms, from rural micro-entrepreneurs to multinational enterprises, are affected, although infrastructure problems usually affect smaller firms the most.

An essential element of policies to promote inclusive and green growth. Reliable and sustainable infrastructure enhances economic activity and contributes to poverty reduction by raising labour productivity, lowering production and transaction costs, as well as reducing social and environmental costs. In order to maximise the contribution of infrastructure to development goals, countries need to build comprehensive infrastructure strategies, support the involvement of low income population and other user groups throughout the planning and implementation phases, emphasise the crucial role of maintenance and sustainability in delivering results, and support the diverse mix of financial instruments facilitating a broader involvement of all providers.

Assessing infrastructure needs and strengthening infrastructure planning. Decisions on how much, where and what kind of infrastructure to build and maintain in order to meet socio-economic and sustainable development trends are complex. Governments need procedures to decide how much to spend on infrastructure, where to allocate spending, including among different infrastructure modes, and how to administer it. This requires a capability to undertake cost-benefit analyses and sound decision-making processes that give weight to the results of those analyses, while allowing a socially acceptable balancing of competing interests. This also requires adequate co-ordination across agencies and at all levels of government, including at the regional level, to identify infrastructure needs across sectors and prioritise projects in accordance with overall development goals and in an integrated manner. Extensive stakeholder consultations with all concerned parties, including end-users, donors, private sector participants, civil society and affected communities, on policy objectives and on individual projects is also key to align objectives and ensure that infrastructure priorities and projects benefit all parts of society.

Prioritising infrastructure projects and deciding on the procurement path. Both the selection of infrastructure projects and the choice between public and private provision should be guided by an impartial assessment of what best serves the public interest. This is best achieved through full cost-benefit analysis taking into account the entire project lifetime, all alternative modes of delivery, the full system of infrastructure provision, and the availability of finance to ensure value for money. All relevant aspects of sustainable development should also be taken into account, including through environmental and social impact assessments, and incorporating climate resilience considerations. Governments may wish to compare the different delivery modes against an objective "public sector comparator" or equivalent, i.e. the conventional public delivery option, when assessing which is likely to deliver the most value for money. Careful sensitivity and risk analysis is necessary to help strike an adequate balance of risk allocation between public and private partners. All short and long-term fiscal risks shouldered by the government, including contingent liabilities, should feature in the cost-benefit analysis and be managed transparently in the budget process. Private participation should not be used as a vehicle for escaping budgetary discipline, and should be pursued only when it is expected to deliver higher value for money. Having gateway mechanisms in the procurement system may help ensure that the chosen form of procurement and the retained modality of private participation are indeed those that secure the best value for money.

Why consider private sector participation in infrastructure provision? Current infrastructure gaps, economic development and growing urbanisation in developing countries, and ageing infrastructures in developed ones, will rapidly strain existing infrastructure and will require not only significant amount of investments but also investment in more efficient and sustainable infrastructure modes. The public sector has traditionally been the main investor in infrastructure and public sources of capital, including at the municipal level where large infrastructure demand lies, will continue to play a crucial role. Nonetheless, meeting these needs is likely to require mobilising additional sources of capital. The private sector can also bring other additional benefits. It can help enhance value for money in the use of public finances for infrastructure development, by expanding the choices of infrastructure delivery, including the bundling of different stages of infrastructure projects, which can lead to cost and efficiency gains. Governments may also benefit from more efficient risk allocation, increased competition and private sector managerial and technological skills. In a number of countries, when adequately regulated and managed, private participation in infrastructure has helped boost both the coverage and efficiency of services.

Signalling government commitment to infrastructure development. Securing necessary resources for infrastructure development, and making infrastructure networks attractive for private participation, are made easier when infrastructure policy priorities and medium to long-term goals are clearly stated and fully embedded in the country's economic development strategies. In this respect, comprehensive national infrastructure plans, identifying a credible pipeline of infrastructure projects across sectors aligned with development objectives, and communicating priorities and the roles expected from the public and private sector, can help secure greater policy co-ordination and alignment across levels of government and assure investors of the government's long-term political commitment to infrastructure development. Establishing a credible pipeline of projects is also likely to attract more investors and facilitate competition for the market. It allows potential investors to build their strategies upon a sizeable portfolio of opportunities rather than on a project-by-project basis, thereby allowing the amortisation of some of the costs associated with assessing infrastructure opportunities in the country. On some occasions, the bundling of small infrastructure projects may also help enhance the attractiveness for long-term investors. Several aspects of trade policies may also contribute to an enabling environment for infrastructure investment, notably by facilitating the import of goods, services, and personnel sometimes needed to adequately and efficiently deliver on infrastructure projects (see the section on *Trade Policy*).

Predictable economic regulation. Establishing a credible institutional and regulatory environment to reduce policy uncertainty is also critical to induce investments. Infrastructure providers will tend to underinvest in the presence of regulatory uncertainty. Investment in infrastructure, and particularly private participation in infrastructure, is made easier where governments implement appropriate institutional arrangements for improving regulatory predictability, including by entrusting regulation and price-setting to specialised authorities that are competent, well-resourced and shielded from undue influence by the parties to infrastructure contracts. Regulatory independence is necessary to insulate regulatory decisions both from the political process and from potential undue influence from infrastructure operators.

A clear legal regime to safeguard investor rights. The legal and institutional framework should facilitate contract enforcement and the functioning of infrastructure partnerships. Infrastructure projects are long-term and are natural candidates for contract renegotiations due to the variability of underlying economic conditions over the project lifetime. The number of failed public-private partnerships in infrastructure sectors attests to the difficult challenges facing policy makers and investors in this respect. Regular consultation with the private partner and stakeholders may help prevent potential conflicts from escalating. Predictable frameworks, including at the contract level, governing the circumstances under which renegotiations shall be considered, can help ensure the flexibility needed for the success of long-term infrastructure contracts. At the same time, the regime for infrastructure procurement and PPPs needs to guard against deliberate understating of project costs – followed by ex-post cost escalation – by private sector bidders. The investment regime needs also to protect core investor rights, including by guaranteeing access to timely and fair compensation in cases of expropriation, and allowing access to dispute settlement mechanisms (see section on *Investment Policy*).

Competition in infrastructure procurement. Savings from more competitive procurement practices can represent a large share of total project development costs. A well-designed procurement regime guarantees procedural fairness to all bidding investors and minimises the risk of corruption, bidder collusion and bid-rigging. Close collaboration among the competition authority, law enforcement authorities responsible for enforcing corruption offences, and public procurement agencies can help to avoid anticompetitive behaviour in the design of bid specifications and in the award of public infrastructure contracts. Specifying contracts in terms of output-based services to be provided to the public and publicising decisions in terms of careful and verifiable references to those criteria adds transparency and helps prevent corruption, besides encouraging companies to propose more innovative and efficient solutions. Simplified procurement procedures, including through electronic systems, may help ease the process, increase competition, and facilitate participation by small-scale bidders – but any simplification should not come at the cost of due diligence and careful contract selection. It needs to ensure that selected bidders have the capacity to deliver upon the contractual commitments throughout the project lifetime.

A competitive market structure. Elements of natural monopoly throughout the infrastructure sector make it more difficult to establish conditions for effective competition. But the benefits of private sector participation are enhanced by efforts to create a competitive environment, including by subjecting activities to appropriate commercial pressures, while subjecting areas of monopoly or scant competition to regulation in the public interest. While many countries have made progress in dismantling barriers to entry in infrastructure sectors, including to foreign investors, progress has not been uniform. FDI restrictions continue to constrain foreign investment in infrastructure sectors in a number of jurisdictions. An open and non-discriminatory regime can widen the number of potential participants and exert pressure on infrastructure providers to perform efficiently. Close co-ordination between regulatory and competition agencies is necessary, particularly in assessing the costs and benefits of unbundling network industries, dismantling unnecessary barriers to entry, and implementing and enforcing adequate competition laws, including to guard against anti-competitive behaviour by incumbents (see section on *Competition Policy*).

Governance of state-owned infrastructure operators. Where privately-owned infrastructure providers coexist with state-owned incumbents, particular measures to maintain a level playing field may also be needed to safeguard a healthy competitive environment and reduce concerns over regulatory discretion and risks, including corruption. Adopting strong corporate governance standards for state-owned enterprises and ensuring that all relevant laws and regulations applicable to private companies also apply to them, including for bankruptcy and competition, and laws prohibiting corrupt acts, help ensure they operate on an equal footing with the private sector (see section on *Corporate Governance*).

Balancing affordability and cost-recovery in price-setting. Countries are also reforming their regulatory regimes to balance cost-recovery needs of public and private investors on the one hand, and end-user affordability on the other. Where cost-recovery prices have been possible and politically acceptable, investment has often substantially increased. When affordability is low, public subsidisation may be necessary. The effectiveness and duration of such subsidies, as well as their weight on the public purse, should be regularly assessed taking into account the performance and efficiency of providers. Smart consumption subsidies instead of production subsidies can help enhance affordability without reducing operators' incentives to perform, but their impact needs to be regularly assessed. To conduct the necessary analyses and make pricing decisions accordingly, it is crucial for infrastructure markets to be overseen by regulatory agencies that have sufficient scope of action, clear lines of accountability, and independence from line ministries as well as from infrastructure incumbents (especially if state-owned). Dedicated funds have also been used to finance universal service requirements imposed on operators.

Inclusiveness and responsible business conduct in infrastructure projects. By connecting firms and people to markets and information, and facilitating access to services that improve people's livelihoods, infrastructure projects can enhance business opportunities, support greater gender equity, and improve the well-being of vulnerable populations. This requires careful upstream preparation of infrastructure projects, with participation of end-users from the outset and with due attention to questions of affordability and inclusion. Moreover, involving end-users, affected communities, private investors and other relevant stakeholders from the earliest stages of infrastructure projects can help ensure that needs and risks are correctly assessed and addressed, and adequately reflected in the contractual structures. Responsible business conduct also helps to ensure infrastructure projects benefit all parts of the society. These projects are often exposed to a number of potential social, economic and environmental risks that need to be addressed, including health, safety and environmental risks associated with large engineering works, but also potential socioeconomic risks related to community resettlement and human rights abuse. The myriad contractual supply relationships these projects involve only amplify these risks. Host and home governments can play a role in encouraging infrastructure providers to observe commonly agreed principles and standards of responsible business conduct (see section on *Policies for Enabling Responsible Business Conduct*).

Stimulating investment in green infrastructure. Infrastructure policies, including pricing policies, should also allow for a level playing field between competing technologies (e.g. between resource-intensive and green technologies) and enable the development of green infrastructure systems, such as sustainable transport infrastructure, renewables-based electricity, climate resilient and energy and resource efficient infrastructure. In managing the transition towards more sustainable modes of infrastructure, governments may benefit, inter alia, from policies re-orienting incentives to green infrastructure delivery, including by removing inefficient fossil-fuel subsidies, and putting a price on carbon emissions and other pollution through market-based instruments. Policies providing long-term financial support and other policies accounting for environmental externalities can also help steer investment towards green infrastructure. These policies are key to address market and regulatory rigidities that may favour incumbent fossil-fuel sources in the electricity sector, for instance; or to help limit private vehicle-based urban sprawl and encourage more sustainable public urban transport systems in metropolitan areas (see section on *Investment Framework for Green Growth*).

Public sector capacity. The success of private involvement in infrastructure also depends on the capacities at all levels of government to deliver on an equal footing with the private sector upon agreed projects and monitor the performance of providers. The lack of private sector experience and technical expertise in government agencies' procurement entities can result in poorly negotiated contracts, inadequate risk management, and costly contract renegotiations. While not a requisite, well-equipped dedicated PPP units with clear mandates and lines of accountability can help enhance project preparation, oversight of procurement processes and the implementation and monitoring performance of infrastructure projects. When available, technical assistance and credit enhancing support from development agencies may also help strengthen project development and implementation capacity, as well as projects' bankability. Monitoring the performance of infrastructure providers at all phases of the project by the relevant government agency and by an independent audit body is also key to ensure value-for-money. Capacity-building efforts, as well as effective stakeholder engagement, also are important to improve the likely success of infrastructure projects.

Regional infrastructure projects. Improved regional connectivity plays an important role in fostering economic integration and growth, including by facilitating firms' integration into global value chains. Where infrastructure projects involve separate jurisdictions, including at the regional level, special caution is warranted to ensure that project objectives are widely shared and underpinned by formal agreements and dispute resolution mechanisms. Regional infrastructure projects require, *inter alia*, shared standards for oversight and transparency of infrastructure procurement processes, including common criteria for bid selection, close co-operation across procuring entities, and agreement on pricing structures and revenue sharing. Having clear and transparent mechanisms for distributing risks and rewards, as well as funding commitments across levels of government is essential for successful regional projects.

Financing for infrastructure. Lastly, access to capital markets to fund operations is essential for infrastructure operators. Taking into account macroeconomic policy conditions, restrictions in access to local markets and obstacles to international capital movements may be phased out to broaden availability of finance. Governments may also benefit from policies to mobilise long-term savings and unlock their use for financing infrastructure investments by long-term institutional investors. In this matter, governments may wish to refer to the *G20/OECD High-Level Principles of Long-Term Investment Financing by Institutional Investors,* which addresses specific regulatory and institutional impediments for long-term investment by institutional investors. Development agencies and export credit agencies can also play an important role in helping countries mobilise additional investment in infrastructure, particularly by channelling resources to enhance the quality of projects, mitigate and clarify risks, and raise the profitability of PPPs.

Core questions and principles

Ensuring coherence and support for infrastructure development

1. Has the government established a comprehensive and integrated infrastructure plan, delineating the government's medium-to-long-term vision and goals, establishing a prioritised and credible pipeline of projects taking into account interactions with other sectors and policy areas and based on adequate initial due diligence? Does it state clearly the expected role, including at sub-sector level, for public and private participation? Does it take into account national and local development objectives and sustainability goals and long-term targets?
2. What processes does the government use to evaluate its infrastructure investment needs and inform infrastructure planning?
3. Does the central government co-operate with local and regional governments, parliamentary bodies and social partners, to establish infrastructure investment priorities and plans? How does it ensure that infrastructure objectives and co-ordination are shared, throughout all levels of government, including at the regional level and in all relevant parts of the public administration, to allow a coherent implementation of the national infrastructure programme?
4. Do authorities consult with end-users and other relevant stakeholders to inform the planning, initiation and operation of infrastructure projects, to ensure that the envisaged undertakings are in the public interest and are acceptable to consumers and other stakeholders?

The enabling environment for investment in infrastructure

5. How is a sound enabling environment for infrastructure investment being created, including a commitment to high standards of public and corporate governance, balanced and transparent procurement procedures, and protection of labour, environmental, property and contractual rights?
6. How is a competitive environment in infrastructure sectors being created, including by subjecting activities to appropriate commercial pressures, dismantling unnecessary barriers to entry and implementing and enforcing adequate competition laws?
7. How do public authorities ensure that infrastructure projects are free from corruption at all levels and in all project phases, including during the bidding stage?

Mitigating project risk and ensuring value-for-money

8. How does the government assess the suitability of infrastructure projects for private investment and operation, inter alia through mitigating project risk and ensuring value-for-money?
9. Are risks in infrastructure projects adequately identified, including social and environmental risks, and measured and allocated to the contractual party that is best able to assess and control them?

10. How are fiscal discipline and transparency safeguarded when the government shares responsibilities with the private sector in infrastructure projects?
11. Are project implementation and ex-post performance systematically audited and assessed by an independent body to ensure greater accountability and consistency of outcome with policy objectives?
12. Do the authorities responsible for privately-operated infrastructure projects (both national and local) have the "ability to deliver", including the capacity to adequately prepare, select and implement infrastructure projects and to partner on an equal basis with their private sector counterparts?
13. To what extent are contractual obligations between public authorities and private sector participants specified in terms of verifiable infrastructure services to be provided to the public (for instance on the basis of output or performance-based specifications)?
14. How are circumstantial changes occurring over the project lifecycle accommodated in the implementation of long-term infrastructure contracts?

Regulation and pricing of infrastructure markets

15. Are the regulatory agencies that oversee infrastructure markets well-equipped in terms of mandates, resources and staff and shielded from undue political interference?
16. Does tariff-setting strike the balance between the imperative of end-user affordability and the need for cost-recovery by the infrastructure operator?
17. How does the government find the appropriate mix of tariffs, taxes and transfers (primarily official development assistance) to establish infrastructure sectors on a financially sustainable basis and ensure social objectives are met? How does it ensure predictability of public fiscal support and subsidies for infrastructure projects and that the fiscal costs of any public subsidisation are proportional with the secured results (in terms of infrastructure delivery or consumer access)?

A balanced market structure for infrastructure provision

18. What is the extent of structural separation different in infrastructure markets? Which authorities are responsible for assessing and making decisions as regards structural separation?
19. Where private providers coexist with state-owned incumbents, how is an adequate level of competition among infrastructure providers assured? How are corporate governance standards of state-owned enterprises being strengthened so as to increase operational efficiency and ensure transparency and accountability?
20. How does the government ensure that small-scale infrastructure service providers are not excluded from infrastructure markets?

Financing infrastructure projects

21. Are infrastructure projects assessed against the degree to which costs can be recovered from end-users and, in case of shortfalls, what other sources of finance can be mobilised to ensure that authorities' targets for service coverage and affordability are met?
22. Has the government enacted policies and regulations to promote long-term savings and to unlock these sources for infrastructure financing? Is official development assistance used to mitigate project risks and leverage private investment in infrastructure?

23. Do private sector participants, including contractors and other financial intermediaries, have adequate access to capital markets to fund operations, and are restrictions in access to local markets and obstacles to international capital movements being progressively phased out, taking into account prudential macroeconomic considerations?

Encouraging inclusiveness and responsible business conduct

24. How do central and local authorities maximise the contribution of infrastructure investment to development, including by ensuring broad-based stakeholder consultations on the reference and impact of infrastructure projects, ex ante poverty impact assessments of competing proposals, and environmental and social impact assessments?
25. How does the government ensure that infrastructure policies and practices reflect sustainable development concerns, including climate change and disaster resistance and contributions to building community resilience?
26. How does the government ensure that public and private sector participants involved in providing vital services to communities effectively observe responsible business conduct standards, including on labour and the environmental, and identify, manage and monitor the associated risks?

Supplemental questions

Ensuring coherence and support for infrastructure development	• Has the government identified areas of over or underinvestment in infrastructure markets? What are the investment needs in each infrastructure sector, including for new investment and operations and maintenance? • Are the powers and responsibilities of national and sub-national entities directly or indirectly involved in infrastructure policy, planning or implementation clear and well-defined in order to facilitate co-ordination and a coherent implementation of the national infrastructure development plan? • Do public authorities communicate clearly the objectives of their infrastructure policies and have in place mechanisms for consultations and full disclosure between the public and private partners regarding specified objectives and individual projects? • To what extent do infrastructure investment needs integrate green policy objectives? What is the estimated investment needed in green infrastructure? • How does the government's strategy to promote private investment in infrastructure take into account the overall green infrastructure goals, notably to develop climate-resilient and energy- and resource-efficient infrastructure systems?
	Sector-specific considerations
	• Particularly in infrastructure sectors which are often conducted at sub-national level, such as water and sanitation and local transport, how does the government ensure policy coherence between the national policy and sub-national activity? • What processes are followed to inform decisions on the development of new transport facilities, as well as the maintenance of existing transport infrastructure? • Are the requirements for all modes of transport regularly reviewed, taking into account investor needs and the links between different modes of transport infrastructure? • How does the government support the shift to sustainable transport modes and trip efficiency in urban transport systems to avoid locking-in carbon-intensive and climate-vulnerable development pathways, as well as to reduce the environmental impact of transport (e.g. through dedicated bus lanes; light-rail transport systems; rapid-transit systems, and alternative transport such as cycling)? • Are there policies to reduce the need to travel by improving transport system efficiency through integrated land-use planning and transport demand management (e.g. through compact, mixed-use urban development, traffic restrictions, or reduction of urban sprawl)? • Are clean energy policies part of a broader national infrastructure framework? Is procurement for new clean energy generation part of a long-term grid infrastructure development strategy? • Has the government evaluated the investment needs in water and sanitation required to support its development goals? Is the private sector involved in water management, supply and infrastructure financing? To what extent does the government approach towards developing water and sanitation infrastructure build on an integrated water resources management policies and practices?

The enabling environment for investment in infrastructure	• What is the overall policy and institutional framework for private investment in infrastructure and how has it been informed by international good practices? • Does the government have a strategy for public-private partnerships, and if so are its provisions and institutions consistent with the broader regime for infrastructure procurement? Does the legal basis for PPPs avoid conflicts with other legislation, either through a PPP act or through sectoral legislation explicitly admitting PPP delivery modes? • Is an open and non-discriminatory investment environment in place for infrastructure providers, including between foreign and domestic and new providers and incumbents? What are the restrictions on foreign investment in infrastructure sectors, if any? To what extent are foreign private companies able to compete on an equal basis with both domestic companies and foreign state-supported companies in seeking access to infrastructure markets? • What modalities for private investment in infrastructure does the government promote? What are the most common concession/PPP modalities across sectors? Is the combined procurement of design, construction and long-term operation allowed? Is the bundling of small infrastructure projects possible in order to minimise transaction costs and thus facilitate attracting investors? Are concession contracts allowed to include no-compete (or exclusivity) clauses? Please describe the main characteristics of licences and concessions. • How do regulatory agencies and the competition authority co-ordinate in assessing the costs and benefits of unbundling network industries and ensuring adequate competition in infrastructure markets? • To what extent do regulatory and competition authorities have adequate political support and independence to denounce anti-competitive behaviour by infrastructure providers (including by SOEs), particularly when challenging vested interests? • Are there clear and transparent guidelines to ensure predictability and consistency in selecting, preparing and procuring infrastructure projects? Are the institutional roles and responsibilities of agencies responsible for these different phases clearly identified in the legal framework? Are these agencies adequately staffed in number and skills to allow the agency to work at the level required by the industry? • Are there regulations to guarantee full disclosure of all project-relevant information between public authorities and their private partners, including on the state of pre-existing infrastructure? • What forms of infrastructure procurement exist and subject to what conditions? When unsolicited proposals are permitted, are there distinct, clear and transparent selection procedures for such proposals? To what extent do existing procedures adequately address the specific transparency issues such proposals entail? • Are there any preference margins for domestic versus foreign bidders, or for SMEs versus larger bidders, in infrastructure procurement procedures? If so, what is the extent of these margins and do they vary according to the sector and size of the project? • What role does the government play in ensuring that corruption is not involved in the procurement process? What steps have been taken to minimise the risk of bid-rigging in infrastructure contracts? • Are competition authorities involved in the procurement process, and how? How are the responsibilities co-ordinated between procurement agencies and the competition authority? • Do selection procedure ensure appropriate due diligence of bidders to assess the realism of the bids, their financial soundness, risk profile and prior experience? Do procedures adequately address any potential conflict of interest? • Are authorities legally required to set and publicise the criteria according to which infrastructure providers will be chosen when an invitation to tender is made? Are the performance standards required from winning bidders carefully defined and publicised in advance of tenders? • Are authorities required publicly to explain award decisions in terms of careful and verifiable references to those criteria? Can bidders challenge the decision by the awarding authority in an independent tribunal? • Are the cost-benefit assessments and the ranking of different projects of a tendering process made public? • What dispute resolution mechanisms exist to ensure that disputes arising at any point in the lifetime of an infrastructure project are handled in a timely and impartial manner?
Mitigating project risk and ensuring value-for-money	• Are decisions to invest in infrastructure projects based on cost-benefit analysis taking into account all alternative modes of delivery, the full system of infrastructure provision, and realistic projections of financial and non-financial costs and benefits over the project lifecycle? When assessing overall costs and benefits, are social and environmental impact assessments mandatory and taken into account? • Does the government systematically assess value-for-money across different delivery modes, including of PPPs and concessions, against a "public sector comparator" or equivalent? • Has the government established a clear policy to guide risk allocation? • How does the government identify, price and manage any risks and contingent liability remaining in hands of the public sector in infrastructure projects undertaken in partnership with the private sector? Are long-term fiscal implications of PPPs accounted for as contingent liabilities in government accounts? Are all the costs and contingent liabilities – including public guarantees on private financing – and the payment stream from government transparently disclosed to the public? • Does the government have (or is it planning to set up) a dedicated PPP expertise unit? What is the line of authority attached to the unit (e.g. independent agency; treasury; Prime Minister/President's cabinet; line ministries)? • Are the institutional roles and responsibilities of agencies responsible for design, negotiation and roll-out of infrastructure procurement (whether using the traditional procurement, the PPP, or the privatisation route) well defined and delineated in legislation? Are there clear lines of authority for who approves what and when throughout the process of project selection, preparation and procurement? • What available channels of communication exist among the PPP Units and different bodies tasked with infrastructure procurement? Do co-ordination issues hamper the effectiveness of PPP development and implementation?

- What steps have been taken to ensure relevant government agencies are adequately staffed, including for the oversight of technical matters and outside contractors, and have the needed financial resources to effectively manage PPP development and implementation? Are there dedicated sources of finance to enhance project preparation (e.g. project development funds for advisory services, pre-feasibility studies, etc.)?
- Do authorities usually obtain environmental licensing and planning permission (e.g. land use change when necessary) before calls for tender are made?
- How is the execution of infrastructure projects involving the private sector facilitated (e.g. standardised contracts; simplified procedures; use of commonly used legal terms)?
- Do contracts provide for the need to accommodate circumstantial changes over the project lifecycle by incorporating explicitly the conditions under which they may be reconsidered or renegotiated? When contracts specify under which circumstances revisions to the original agreement shall be considered, what type of mechanisms are mostly used for such occasional renegotiations to be conducted in good faith, in a transparent and non-discriminatory manner (e.g. permanent and active review panels, dispute committees and arbitrational instances, among other)?
- What other measures are used to limit the possibility of contract renegotiation (e.g. profit-sharing mechanisms; equity participation; compensation rules for early termination; among other)?
- Are regular and timely consultations with contractual partners and stakeholders the norm, or are ad hoc meetings organised when one of the contractual partners or stakeholders perceives a problem? Are affected third parties systematically invited to participate in such consultations?

Regulation and pricing of infrastructure markets

- How is regulation of infrastructure services co-ordinated? Which sectors have a dedicated regulatory agency, and which are overseen by a line ministry? Which authorities have powers to verify regulatory implementation, supervise infrastructure providers, apply fines and sanctions, or set tariffs? Which authorities have the right to issue, enforce and revoke licences in infrastructure sectors?
- Do regulatory agencies make use of performance indicators to systematically monitor infrastructure operators following clear criteria and scheduling defined in contract? Are these publicised? If yes, please indicate in which sectors.
- Is there a system of penalties/ rewards attached with the non-compliance/ good performance of the private partner?
- Is there an independent agency that evaluates PPP performance ex-post (i.e., evaluates the consistency of the PPP outcome with the economic policy objectives set ex-ante, including financial objectives)? Is the Supreme Audit Institution or equivalent public auditor, assessing and auditing project ex-post and reporting to parliamentary bodies, well equipped to perform its activities?
- Do regulatory agencies have clear responsibilities and powers, and are they well-resourced and shielded from undue political influence (and from the influence of parties to the infrastructure contracts concerned)?
- To what extent are regulatory agencies funded from independent sources beyond government influence (e.g. annual fee from regulated companies)? Do the regulatory agencies receive instructions from the executive? Can their decisions be overturned by the executive?
- Are regulatory agencies adequately staffed in number and skills to allow the agency to work at the level required by the industry? Are there any arrangements for technical co-operation with competition authorities? How are responsibilities shared between these agencies?
- Are decision-making rules clear and transparent to ensure predictability and to avoid undue personal influence? Are regulators required to publicise decisions and the explanatory reasons supporting them? Can infrastructure operators appeal administrative decisions?
- What steps have been taken to ensure regulators are accountable for their decisions in view of avoiding opportunism, corruption and inefficiencies? To whom are regulatory authorities accountable: Parliament, the Executive or a Ministry? Is regulators' performance formally reviewed by independent auditors or legislative committees?
- To what extent, and how, have regulatory agencies or competition authorities addressed anti-competitive practices by incumbent enterprises, including state-owned enterprises (SOEs), including those that inhibit investment in green infrastructure?
- How are infrastructure projects generally financed at the operational stage (user fees, government revenues, or mixed), and how does this vary by sector?
- On what basis are prices in infrastructure markets calculated and how often are they revised? Are there regulated prices, entirely or partially? How are regulated prices determined (e.g. cost-based pricing, such as pre-determined rate of return, or incentives-based pricing, such as price-caps, or other form of regulation)? If price-caps are used, how are these set?
- To what extent are prices allowed to vary according to consumption behaviour and customer's socio-economic characteristics?
- When public subsidisation is socially necessary, what steps have been taken to ensure it is set at an optimal level, taking into account the need to meet socially desired objectives (e.g. access expansion or affordability concerns) while continuing to encourage the efficient delivery of infrastructure providers?
- How important is public subsidisation: what is the gap between the average tariff and average cost of services unit in each infrastructure sectors? What is the share of infrastructure subsidies as a percentage of GDP or budget, and is this regularly made public?

Sector-specific considerations

- In the telecommunications sector, how are interconnection and access prices determined? To what extent are they cost-oriented?

	• In the transport sector, has the government implemented adequate pricing mechanisms taking into account the full costs of fossil-fuel based road transport and shifted incentives away from carbon-intensive road transport (e.g. carbon pricing; fuel and vehicle taxes; reform of fossil-fuel subsidies; congestion charges and other road user charges; parking levies, etc.)? • What are the major forms of electrification (e.g. grid, off-grid and mini-grid)? Are private sector captive users allowed to sell power back to the grid? Does the sector regulatory agency have authority over all or only some forms of electrification? • In energy generation, to what extent are primary input prices determined by the market or negotiated? Are any automatic pricing mechanisms used? • For both energy and water sectors, how are tariffs determined? What is the structure of tariffs (e.g. flat or time-differentiated tariffs)? Does the dominant infrastructure operator have a say in revising the tariff, or does the regulator have an independent methodology for cost assessment and tariff revision? • What steps have been taken to bring prices closer to cost-recovery levels? What portion of the overall cost of providing the service is covered through tariffs? • How are the costs for different services allocated between consumers in view of affordability (geographic or industry-specific tariffs, increasing block tariffs, stepped tariffs, etc.)? Are any non-tariff mechanisms used (e.g. coupons or targeted income support)? • Is the effect of production and consumption subsidies, as well as the fiscal cost, regularly assessed and reported on? • Has the government taken measures to remove inefficient fossil-fuel subsidies? Are the level and efficiency of these subsidies monitored on a regular basis? • As water is linked, inter alia, to agriculture, food security and health, how do the government and donor partners work together to develop and use integrated water resource management frameworks and strengthen co-ordination between central and decentralised levels of government?
Financing infrastructure investment*	• What sort of long-term investment vehicles are available to mobilise funds for infrastructure? • Is there a robust project finance market which supplements the traditional corporate finance market? • What steps have been taken to ensure the domestic capital market is conducive to long-term investment? Have specific policies been enacted to support the development of project bonds? • How does the government ensure co-ordination of policies and regulations in the financial system in order to avoid potentially unintended consequences for the financing of infrastructure projects as a result of new regulations aimed at financial stability? • Do current regulations and rules support investments in infrastructure projects by long-term investors, including pension and equity funds? Are there efforts to ease regulatory barriers preventing greater resource allocation to infrastructure projects by institutional investors? • Has the government established special purpose funds for infrastructure maintenance and for addressing social objectives such as universal service provision? How are these financed? • Is the government working with donors to provide more predictable and long term support for infrastructure? How does it benefit from official development assistance (ODA)? To what extent has ODA been used to improve financial viability of infrastructure projects while taking into account poor people's ability to pay? Are ODA resources from donors well-co-ordinated with other sources of infrastructure finance, such as export credit agencies? • What sort of financial instruments and mechanisms are in place to stimulate private investment in green infrastructure, including attracting long-term institutional investment (e.g. green bonds, carbon finance mechanisms, etc.)? • What types of incentives (e.g. subsidies, tax exemptions and feed-in tariffs) are in place to stimulate private investment in support of green infrastructure goals? Are incentives time-limited and appropriately targeted? (see section on *Tax Policy* for guidance on tax incentives) **Sector-specific considerations** • Are there any incentives for investment in clean energy infrastructure? Who bears the costs of such incentives (e.g. taxpayers, customers, providers of CO_2 credits)? • Have carbon and other pollution emissions been priced? Is the price set in a transparent and predictable manner? How is the price level determined? Is there a market mechanism (tax or cap-and-trade systems) to price carbon and other pollutants?
Balanced market structure for private participation in infrastructure	• Which parts of network industries have been open to market competition or competitive tendering? Which markets remain dominated by SOEs? • Is there a national code of corporate governance, and if so, does it have a chapter/ section (or a separate code) dedicated to corporate governance of SOEs? • Does it establish a clear separation between the public sector's ownership function and other factors that may influence companies' position, service obligations, access to finance and weight on the public purse? • To what extent are SOEs exempt from the application of general laws and regulations (e.g. competition and bankruptcy legislation)? When this is the case, has the government taken steps to ensure this is minimised to the fullest extent possible in order to avoid market distortions? • Are SOEs, regardless of their legal status and even if not listed, regularly audited by independent auditors? Are they required to disclose financial and non-financial information according to high quality international accounting and financial reporting standards?

	• Are the obligations and responsibilities of SOEs clearly mandated by laws or regulations? Are the related fiscal costs, as well as the SOE's economic performance, disclosed to the general public in a transparent manner – and by what agency? **Sector-specific considerations** • In the telecommunications sector, do authorities assess market access potential and the extent of competition among operators? • What are the main characteristics of telecom licences: multi-service licensing allowed; technology-and-service neutral rules; universal access obligations; etc.? Are there clear rules for network sharing? Is number portability allowed? • In the electricity sector, what is the degree of integration from power generation to power supply (e.g. unbundling, independent power provision under the 'single-buyer model' etc.)? • What efforts have been taken to the development of diversified off-grid energy infrastructure, as well as feed-in infrastructure? If feed-in tariffs are allowed, how are these determined? When and on what basis is the price of the tariff susceptible to change? If tenders for clean energy are used, how are bidders selected and prices determined in the tender? • To what extent does the clean energy sector face higher barriers to foreign investment? Do foreign investors face limiting constraints such as local content requirements? If so, what are the objectives behind these measures and is the government considering alternative ways of achieving these objectives?
Enhancing regional connectivity and supply chains	• In what ways is the government involved in promoting cross-border infrastructure investment to enhance regional connectivity and the integration into regional supply chains? Please indicate any cross-border infrastructure projects in which your country is involved, including regional power pools, shared river basins and hydropower projects etc. • In the case of cross-border infrastructure projects, do the involved governments commit ex-ante to a sufficient allocation of budgetary resources, and agree on shared development priorities to be upheld throughout the project? • Should a dispute or need for contract re-negotiation arise in a cross-border project, what is the competent jurisdiction and how will the dispute be resolved? • To what extent are pricing structures aligned among countries engaged in a cross-border project (for instance, alignment of national pricing structures to facilitate cross-border power purchase agreements; or agreement on levels of road tolling on either side of the border)?
Encouraging inclusiveness and responsible business conduct	• What strategies are in place for communicating and consulting with the general public, including vis-à-vis consumers, affected communities and corporate stakeholders, with a view to developing mutual acceptance and understanding of the objectives of the parties involved in infrastructure projects? • Do public authorities work together with private actors, and affected communities, to avoid and mitigate environmental and socially unacceptable outcomes? • What are the existing frameworks and capacity to address potential environmental emergencies associated with infrastructure development (e.g. dams, liquid natural gas terminals, pipeline, etc.) • How does the procuring agency, the regulatory agency or the competition authority ensure that infrastructure providers, be they public or private, act according to the norms of responsible business conduct as mentioned in the OECD Guidelines for Multinational Enterprises (see section on *Policies for Enabling Responsible Business Conduct*)? • How does the government encourage local private sector provision of services and the development of local industries for construction and maintenance of infrastructure assets? • Does the government facilitate SME participation in infrastructure contracts (for instance by simplifying bidding procedures for SMEs, setting quotas for a minimum number of SMEs to participate in the bidding process, sub-dividing infrastructure contracts etc.)? • What specific approaches are in place to deal with the particularities of fragile and post conflict zones, including the importance of core infrastructure and of building governance and administrative capacity? **Sector-specific considerations** • How does the government seek to link ICT infrastructure programmes with activities in other sectors important for the livelihoods of poor people? • How does the government support grid extensions in areas less attractive to operators but necessary from a social perspective? How does it balance costs, revenues and the need for smart subsidies?

* Please refer to the *G20/OECD High-Level Principles of Long-Term Investment Financing by Institutional Investors* and *Checklist* for specific guidance on policies to facilitate and promote long-term investment in infrastructure by institutional investors.

Additional resources

Websites

OECD, *Water Infrastructure Investment*, *www.oecd.org/daf/inv/investment-policy/water.htm*.

OECD, *Clean Energy Infrastructure Investment*, *www.oecd.org/daf/inv/investment-policy/clean-energy-infrastructure.htm*.

OECD, *Institutional Investors and Long-Term Investment*, *www.oecd.org/fr/finances/pensions-privees/institutionalinvestorsandlong-terminvestment.htm*.

OECD, *Public-Private Partnerships*, *www.oecd.org/gov/budgeting/ppp.htm*.

World Bank, Public-Private Infrastructure Advisory Facility (PPIAF), *www.ppiaf.org/*.

References, tools, guidance, manuals

Ang, G. and V. Marchal (2013), "Mobilising Private Investment in Sustainable Transport: The Case of Land-Based Passenger Transport Infrastructure", *OECD Environment Working Papers*, No. 56, OECD Publishing, Paris, *http://dx.doi.org/10.1787/5k46hjm8jpmv-en*.

G20/OECD (2014), *Checklist on Long-Term Investment Financing Strategies and Institutional Investors*, OECD Paris, *https://g20.org/wp-content/uploads/2014/12/8%20G20-OECD%20Checklist %20on%20Long-Term%20Investment%20Financing%20Strategies%20and%20Institutional%20 Investors.pdf*.

G20/OECD (2012), *High-Level Principles of Long-Term Investment Financing by Institutional Investors*, OECD Paris, *www.oecd.org/finance/private-pensions/G20-OECD-Principles-LTI-Financing.pdf*.

OECD (2015), *Fostering investment in infrastructure: lessons learned from OECD Investment Policy Reviews*, OECD Paris, *www.oecd.org/daf/inv/investment-policy/Fostering-Investment-in-Infrastructure.pdf*.

OECD (2014), *Policy Guidance for Investment in Clean Energy Infrastructure: expanding access to clean energy for green growth and development*, OECD Paris, available at: *www.oecd.org/daf/inv/investment-policy/CleanEnergyInfrastructure.pdf*.

OECD (2012), *Principles for Public Governance of Public-Private Partnerships*, OECD Paris, *www.oecd.org/governance/budgeting/PPP-Recommendation.pdf*.

OECD (2012), *Recommendation on Regulatory Policy and Governance*, OECD Paris, *www.oecd.org/governance/regulatory-policy/49990817.pdf*.

OECD (2011), *Competition Assessment Toolkit: Principles*, OECD Paris, available at: *www.oecd.org/daf/competition/46193173.pdf*.

OECD (2011), *Meeting the Challenge of Financing Water and Sanitation: Tools and Approaches*, OECD Studies on Water, OECD Paris, *http://dx.doi.org/10.1787/9789264120525-en*.

OECD (2011), *Guidelines for Performance-Based Contracts between Water Utilities and Municipalities: Lessons learnt from Eastern Europe, Caucasus and Central Asia*, OECD Paris, *www.oecd.org/env/resources/49092291.pdf*.

OECD (2009), *Principles for Integrity in Public Procurement*, OECD Paris, *www.oecd.org/gov/ethics/48994520.pdf*.

OECD (2009), *Guidelines for Fighting Bid Rigging in Public Procurement*, OECD Paris, *www.oecd.org/competition/cartels/42851044.pdf*.

OECD (2009), *Principles for Private Sector Participation in Infrastructure*, OECD Paris, *www.oecd.org/daf/inv/investment-policy/38309896.pdf*.

OECD (2009), *Private Sector Participation in Water Infrastructure: OECD Checklist for Public Action*, OECD Paris, *www.oecd.org/investment/investment-policy/42347077.pdf*.

OECD (2006), "DAC Guiding Principles on Using Infrastructure to Reduce Poverty", in OECD (2006), *Promoting Pro-Poor Growth: Infrastructure*, OECD Paris, *www.oecd.org/development/povertyreduction/36301078.pdf*.

OECD (2005), *OECD Guidelines on Corporate Governance of State-Owned Enterprises*, OECD Paris, *www.oecd.org/corporate/ca/corporategovernanceofstate-ownedenterprises/34803211.pdf*.

OECD (2005), *OECD Guiding Principles for Regulatory Quality and Performance*, OECD Paris, *www.oecd.org/fr/reformereg/34976533.pdf*.

OECD (2002), *OECD Best Practices for Budget Transparency*, OECD Paris, *www.oecd.org/governance/budgeting/Best%20Practices%20Budget%20Transparency%20-%20complete%20with %20cover%20page.pdf*.

OECD (2001), *Recommendation of the Council Concerning Structural Separation in Regulated Industries*, OECD Paris, *www.oecd.org/regreform/sectors/25315195.pdf*.

United Nations (2004), *UNCITRAL – Model Legislative Provisions on Privately Financed Infrastructure Projects*, United Nations: New York, *www.uncitral.org/pdf/english/texts/procurem/pfip/model/03-90621_Ebook.pdf*.

Indicators

OECD, *Indicators of Product Market Regulation*, *www.oecd.org/economy/growth/indicatorsofproductmarketregulationhomepage.htm#indicators*.

OECD, *FDI Regulatory Restrictiveness Index*, *www.oecd.org/investment/fdiindex.htm*.

World Bank Private Participation in Infrastructure Database, *http://ppi.worldbank.org/*.

Policy Framework for Investment
2015 Edition

10. Financing investment

The financial system performs many functions necessary for broad-based economic activity. It allocates credit and resources efficiently, handles payments (both domestically and internationally via currency exchanges), collects and disseminates information (especially on asset prices), facilitates maturity transformation and manages liquidity, market and other forms of risks. Well-functioning financial systems are important for economic growth by providing funding for capital accumulation and by helping to allocate resources to their best uses. Increased capital accumulation can, in turn, have long-lasting effects on the rate of economic growth if it has spill-over effects to other factors of production or to productivity. Financial activities in turn require various transactions and information infrastructure to support the entire process, including an appropriate legal and regulatory system, as well as adequate supervision, tax laws, and societal and industry norms.

A comprehensive assessment of financial sector policies and practices is beyond the scope of the *Policy Framework for Investment*. Instead, this section is intended to support discussion of some of the key aspects that policymakers and others concerned with financing investment should take into consideration as one element of a sound environment for investment. The OECD and other international organisations dispose of a range of instruments to support more thorough reviews of countries' financial environment. References to these can be found at the end of the section.

When the financial system works as it should, it enables growing firms to seize promising investment opportunities, especially small and innovative enterprises that need external funding to expand and develop their businesses. By facilitating new entry into product markets, the financial system helps to impose discipline on firms and boost efficiency, both directly and indirectly by helping better performers to grow and by forcing weaker performers to improve, merge with or be acquired by a stronger firm, or exit. At a more micro level, when access to financial services is extended to the poor, and notably to women in developing countries, whose access to financial services is often more limited, it also helps to reduce poverty and inequality and to improve gender equity.

A key challenge for policymakers is to put in place a policy mix that avoids macroeconomic imbalances and financial sector vulnerabilities that can thwart the growth process. Macroeconomic stability is a necessary condition for savings mobilisation and credit expansion and for overall financial deepening. Appropriate regulation and supervision of financial sectors, as well as high quality corporate governance standards, are crucial for limiting excessive risk-taking by economic agents, while encouraging the development of more resilient financial systems. The 2008 global financial crisis highlighted the risks poorly regulated and supervised financial systems can pose to financial stability and to economic growth and development.

Economic exchange, in general, and financial transactions in particular, depend on trust and confidence, which can be difficult to restore once lost. Investors are willing to commit their funds only when they have some assurance that financial markets and institutions are safe and sound, and operate according to rules and procedures that are fair, transparent and free from conflicts of interest and other agency problems. Investment integrity requires adequate regulation, disclosure, accountability and better financial education and training to facilitate proper risk assessment. Institutions will be reluctant to invest if risks are not clearly understood and rewards are not sufficient, a determination which can only be made confidently if relevant risk factors are transparently communicated to allow them to be properly assessed and priced (see the section on *Corporate Governance*).

Adequate regulation and supervision is also necessary to safeguard consumer interests in relation to financial products and to guide and promote action by financial institutions with respect to responsible business conduct. Responsible business conduct can be a tool for risk management as well as a means of driving value, as strong environmental and social governance has been positively linked with financial performance. Expectations are growing for the financial sector to adopt a comprehensive due diligence approach as a part of responsible business conduct, including to assess and address social and environmental risks related to operations and business relationships in addition to commercial risks as reflected in the OECD *Guidelines for Multinational Enterprises* (see the section on *Policies for Enabling Responsible Business Conduct*).

Governments can also support the growth, and facilitate the financing of, investments by ensuring that investors and creditors have clearly defined rights and can enforce them. A strong legal environment and effective enforcement capabilities are especially important for access to external finance. These rights need to be well balanced. When creditor rights are weak and contract enforcement is long and costly, financial intermediaries will be less willing to extend credit to firms. When shareholder rights are weak, investors will be less willing to extend equity finance. Having efficient enforcement mechanisms in place also facilitates the development of asset-based financing (e.g. factoring, leasing, and securitisation). This also requires effective insolvency regimes that allow viable firms to reorganise and unviable ones to efficiently exit the market, and that ensure the orderly resolution of debts incurred by debtors. An efficient and modern framework should allow for a clear and transparent process for reorganising troubled businesses and expedited bankruptcy procedures.

Inadequate legal and regulatory environments governing property rights can make banks and other financial institutions reluctant to accept movable assets as collateral, which can be particularly important in the case of small and medium-sized enterprises (SMEs). Well-defined property rights can enable individuals and firms to borrow on a longer-term basis and at a lower cost. A well-developed legal framework in this manner should support the use of all kinds of assets and rights as collateral, including movable property, while as far as possible eliminating formal requirements to create collateral, and should foster transparency and predictability for commercial transactions.

The government may also seek to ensure that the legal framework is supported by publicly open, affordable and efficient registry systems. Well-functioning registry systems allow parties to ascertain any already existing security interest over registered property and establish the priority of creditors vis-à-vis third parties. The lack of reliable information on the creditworthiness of potential borrowers, often due to inappropriate accounting records and lack of collateral, prevents lenders from properly assessing risks, leading to higher interest rates or limited credit. SMEs can be particularly disadvantaged relative to larger and more established firms in this regard. Their difficulty in obtaining financing will be compounded when the business environment lacks transparency, when the legal system is weak, when monopolies are present, and when regulations might unintentionally discourage lenders from financing SMEs.

Improving the availability of information through public credit registries or private credit bureaus helps to facilitate credit expansion, notably in developing economies, even when creditors' rights and enforcement systems underperform. Governments can create favourable frameworks for credit information collection and dissemination by enacting and enforcing data protection and credit reporting laws, allowing an effective sharing of information and protection of debtors' rights.

These types of legal and regulatory framework conditions for financial systems, particularly their enforcement and transparency, support innovation and investment in new enterprises (see the section on *Investment Promotion and Facilitation*). Even so, direct state interventions to support SME financing may sometimes be necessary, in particular, in cases of market failures and incomplete markets that inhibit the provision of adequate financing or financing on terms suitable for the stage of SME development. Public policies aimed at promoting SMEs should be focused, aimed at making markets work efficiently and sustainably, and at providing incentives for the private sector to assume an active role in SME finance. The principles of risk sharing should guide public programmes, with official contributions encouraging partnership with entrepreneurs, banks, businesses, and universities. Efficient government support schemes ensure "additionality", i.e. that resources are allocated to viable firms partially or completely excluded from the financial market, and prevent excessive risk transfer from the private to the public sector. Increased financial literacy and non-financial assistance, including through capacity building on financial management and business development, can also help SMEs find financing in the market, particularly agricultural SMEs and farmers. In all cases of direct government support, assessments and evaluations should be applied rigorously to phase out policies that have become ineffective or where market activities are maturing and are able to take over.

Establishing these framework conditions is necessary for the proper functioning of the financial system but may not be sufficient to encourage lenders to provide financing to certain types of SMEs, in particular, start-ups and very young firms that typically lack sufficient collateral or to firms whose activities offer the possibility of high returns but at a substantial risk of loss. These activities are candidates for equity-type finance and not credit. Some adjustments may be necessary to encourage the deployment of such patient capital in SME equities. Even in developed economies, the share of SME financing provided through capital markets is very low, despite the existence in some cases of organised exchanges and platforms devoted to small firms. For many venues, liquidity is a key challenge to be overcome. In some jurisdictions further development in the ecosystem (exchanges, platforms, brokers, market-makers, advisors, equity research) is necessary both to develop SME equity finance and to maintain adequate liquidity in such market segments. The lack of a risk equity culture is an obstacle in some cases, which calls for increased education regarding equity investments for all market constituencies (i.e., individual investors, advisors, and SMEs themselves).

Government policy can be useful for addressing some of the illiquidity in growth markets, but rather than relaxing certain listing and reporting requirements for SMEs, governments may instead want to develop proportionate, adapted legislation designed for small (and mid) capitalisation firms. For example, alternative prospectus requirements may be designed with SMEs in mind, as opposed to demoting the level and quality of information provided or sacrificing investor protection.

Financing long-term investments is another especially challenging task, given the longer time horizons of such projects over which agency problems and related weaknesses can materialise, the greater uncertainty regarding investment returns, the illiquidity of certain types of investments, including a lack of both transparency and the data needed to understand the risks of direct investments and alternative financing vehicles used, insufficient investor capacity to manage longer-term assets, and potential problems with investment conditions and market infrastructure (see the section on *Investment in Infrastructure*).

Institutional investors are increasingly looked upon as alternative sources of long-term financing, in particular in light of the tightening liquidity and capital constraints being placed on the banking sector. The government can play a supporting role in developing the institutional investor sector, which can in turn contribute to growth and development of private capital markets. The G20/OECD High-Level Principles for Long-Term Investment Financing by Institutional Investors provides specific guidance on ways governments can facilitate and promote long-term investment by institutional investors.

Governments can potentially help foster long-term investments by improving policy predictability and the efficiency of the use of resources as well as by the direct use of funds, but project support should be given only in circumstances that clearly require it. Given the constraints on government budgets and the considerable need for long-term investment now and in the future, it is essential that governments partner with the private sector to meet some of these needs. The expected return and risk of investment projects is a core consideration in the effort to attract private financing. Government intervention may be needed in some circumstances, where the rate of return may be insufficient to compensate private sector investors for the perceived level and character of risk or to address key market failures that significantly impede the supply of funds. Where appropriate, governments may wish to implement policies supporting the development of Islamic finance, which can also help mobilise long-term capital for development.

Lastly, ensuring the financial system's efficiency is another building block to create a favourable environment for the financing of economic activity. Greater competition, including by allowing foreign participation, generally contributes to developing more efficient banking institutions and helps to enhance financial deepening. Market contestability helps ensure that banks behave competitively thereby helping to mitigate the effects of concentration on access to finance. By contrast, state ownership of banks and regulatory restrictions on lending can exacerbate the negative impact of low competition in the banking sector. Foreign participation in the domestic banking sector may also add to stability and financial development as they can make use of their internal markets in times of host country crisis and of their cross-border experience to introduce innovation.

When the participation of foreign banks is permitted, governments have an interest in allowing them to access local deposit markets to fund their operations, as internationally funded banks may be more likely to reduce lending more dramatically than locally funded banks in the case of shocks to the parent bank. That said, foreign bank presence may also involve costs in certain circumstances, notably in the case of low-income countries and countries with weak institutions. If foreign banks engage in cherry-picking the best clients, this may lead to a worsening of the credit pool remaining for domestic banks, potentially reducing their willingness to lend. This may ultimately deter overall credit provision if credit by foreign banks is offset by reduced credit from domestic banks. Nonetheless, in many cases the presence of foreign banks has been associated with greater access to finance, including by SMEs and both from foreign and domestic banks, which may increase their emphasis on the sector when facing greater competition in the upper segments of the market.

Core questions and principles

1. Has the government established a macroeconomic and business environment and a policy, operational and legal infrastructure for the financial sector conducive to financing investment?
2. What processes does the government use to evaluate the capacity of the financial sector, including the quality of its regulatory framework, to support enterprise development effectively?
3. What laws and regulations are in place to protect the rights of borrowers and creditors and are these rights adequately balanced?
4. Is a registry system in place to support the use of property, including moveable property, as collateral to expand business access to external sources of credit?
5. What data protection and credit reporting laws have been enacted to facilitate the flow of information and improve financial sector stability, thereby enhancing the investment environment?
6. Do laws and regulations provide for an efficient bankruptcy regime and credit-recovery procedures?
7. What measures are in place to ensure financial sector and capital market participants comply with high quality corporate governance standards?
8. How does the government ensure that the laws and regulations dealing with long-term investments and investors and their implementation and enforcement are clear, transparent, widely accessible and do not impose unnecessary burdens?
9. Is there adequate access to bank lending in the economy, including for SMEs?
10. To what extent are financial tools, including insurance, available for enterprises to mitigate financial and other risks linked to their activities, including those operating internationally?
11. To what extent is risk capital available to support early growth and private investment? What measures have been adopted to broaden the range of financing sources available for enterprises beyond traditional bank finance, including with respect to the development of corporate bond and equity markets and access to non-bank financing instruments by SMEs?
12. What steps has the government taken to strengthen competition in the financial sector, including to facilitate the participation of foreign institutions, and to raise the efficiency of financial intermediation?

Supplemental questions

Enabling environment for financing investment

Macroeconomic and business environment

- Does the macroeconomic environment provide the necessary conditions for the development of the financial sector and capital markets, capable of sustaining private investment? Is the macroeconomic environment stable and free of imbalances and financial sector vulnerabilities?
- What growth policies has the government established to support enterprise creation, development, and investment? What is the quality of the business environment – is it conducive to long-term investment and financing? Are financial markets open and competitive? Are there restrictions including caps on foreign equity investments and ownership in the financial sector?

Policy framework for financing investment

- How does the policy and regulatory framework for the financial sector support the development of the financial system in order to enable enterprise development, innovation and sustainable economic growth?
- Does the government have a financial sector development plan to guide the development and enhance the stability and efficiency of the financial sector and its ability to finance investment? What have been the main financial sector reforms implemented to support greater access to finance and promote more efficient financial intermediation? Are future policy reforms envisaged?
- To what extent are regulatory impact assessments used to evaluate the consequences of regulations on the financing environment for business activities?
- How does the framework ensure financial institutions and capital markets observe the principle of responsible business conduct, including responsibility to take appropriate risk-based due diligence and action in order to prevent and mitigate any possible adverse impact arising from its own activities or from its business relationships? To what extent do these measures encourage financial institutions to take into account environmental and social principles in decision-making, both on the investment side and on the procurement and employment side (see section on *Policies for Enabling Responsible Business Conduct*)?
- When Islamic finance is available, what policies have been implemented to develop the sector?

Financial infrastructure

- Has the government made dedicated efforts to establish an efficient and robust financial infrastructure (payment system, trading, settlement, and clearing)?

Legal framework

- What laws and mechanisms are available to ensure expedited reorganisation and bankruptcy of firms, as well as efficient enforcement of creditor's rights and protection of debtor's rights? Does the law provide for out-of-court procedures for seizure and sale of property? Does the regulatory framework provide for public or private enforcement agencies? Are there specialised commercial courts? If not, do judges have any special training to hear complex commercial disputes (see section on *Investment Policy*)?
- Are financial contracts enforceable at low cost and with minimum delay? Is the system of contract enforcement widely accessible to all investors, domestic and foreign? Are these factors comparable with those of other jurisdictions in the region or countries at the same stage of development?
- Has the government taken steps towards the progressive establishment of timely, secure and effective methods of ownership registration for land and other forms of physical property?
- Is a centralised collateral registry in place to efficiently register and inform parties of all claims against property with potential to conflict with the rights of others, including movable property, such as account receivables, inventory and agricultural production? Has the government implemented a web-based or electronic collateral registry to facilitate registration and searches?
- Is there a secured financing law that provides for clear priority rules in view of ensuring claims against movable property are discoverable, predictable and quantifiable?
- Has the government adopted effective data protection and credit reporting laws to enable the flow of credit information and facilitate access to finance? Are there public credit registries and private credit bureaus to provide reliable information? Does the law provide for debtors' right to access their own credit information in a timely manner and for any grievance or dispute resolution mechanisms for them to challenge any information they consider incorrect?
- Are laws and regulations dealing with long-term investment and investors, clear, transparent, widely accessible and not unnecessarily burdensome?
- What measures are in place to ensure that financial sector and capital market participants comply with high quality standards of corporate governance?

Access to bank finance	• To what extent do banks provide financing for enterprises in the economy, in comparison with capital markets? What obstacles, if any, exist with respect to access to bank financing? • Are there regulations or incentives, such guarantee schemes, in place to promote SME lending by banking institutions? Are these initiatives meeting policy objectives? Do they compromise banking sector stability in any way? • Are there programmes or initiatives to build the managerial and financial capacity of entrepreneurs and SMEs in order to facilitate access to finance? Has the government implemented initiatives to develop the financial and business skills of entrepreneurs, and how effective are they? • To what extent does the government promote financial literacy and makes use of financial education programmes as a complement to consumer protection and regulatory reforms in advancing financial inclusion and consumer awareness?
Risk mitigation and insurance	• How well developed are insurance markets, in particular for commercial entities? To what extent do such markets provide coverage against key risks facing enterprises, e.g. property, business interruption, trade credit? • How are risks related to domestic and global supply chains and international trade handled by businesses? What role, if any, do state-owned enterprises and the insurance sector play in mitigating these risks? • (If relevant) Has the government established policies to develop Islamic insurance?
Access to risk capital, capital market financing, and the market for corporate control	• What is the role of the private risk capital industry (e.g. venture capital, mezzanine finance and private equity) in financing growth companies? Has the government sought to increase the role of private risk capital in financing growth? • To what extent do capital markets provide a mechanism for financial intermediation in the economy? What are the respective roles of stock markets and the corporate bond market? Is local currency debt available for long tenors? Is a credit culture being developed based on risk assessment and management? Is a sufficient secondary market available for refinancing debt and for trading equity? What future developments are expected? What are the main policies that have been implemented to support the development of capital markets? What challenges exist? • Can investors raise debt in the local market to finance investments, such as large-scale infrastructure projects? • What measures, if any, have been adopted to facilitate SME access to capital markets, including through dedicated stock exchanges and SME bond markets? • What is the nature of securities market rules governing takeover bids? Do these rules enable an efficient market for corporate control and market discipline? How active is the market for mergers and acquisitions of listed companies? Is the financial system adequately developed to support takeover activity? • Are financial statements prepared by private and publicly traded companies consistent with high quality and internationally accepted accounting and auditing standards? • Is there a diversified investor base for capital market securities? Is there a dominant class of investors (e.g. banks, pension funds, insurers, central banks, etc.)? • What steps have been taken to ensure well-designed legal and regulatory frameworks for various types of institutional investors? What types of institutional investors are supported? Are there direct regulatory constraints on the investment activities of institutional investors? If yes, what is the intended objective of the constraint? • Has the government developed specific policies or strategies to promote increased allocations to long-term investment projects by institutional investors? • What barriers, if any, are there to the participation of institutional investors in SME financing (e.g. debt, equity, or venture financing)? • Has the government established frameworks to support the necessary external service providers such as actuaries, auditors, depositories, trustees, etc.? • Is the issuing and listing of securities particularly complex, costly and cumbersome? What measures have been taken to streamline these and facilitate access to markets? Are there other issuance channels, such as private placement, with lower compliance conditions available for companies to raise funds? • (If relevant) When Islamic finance is available, what policies have been implemented to promote the development of Islamic capital markets, including of debt and equity instruments?
Financial system efficiency	• What policies have been implemented to ensure an adequate level of competition in the financial sector? How does the performance of the banking sector and other financial sectors compare to that of peer economies? • Are foreign established (branches or subsidiaries) financial institutions accorded similar treatment to that of domestically-owned financial institutions with respect to all elements of the regulatory system? Please describe any existent discrimination (see section on *Investment Policy*). • Are there any de jure or de facto barriers on foreign entry for foreign financial institutions, including institutional investors (e.g. foreign equity limitations, or restrictions on branching or on establishing subsidiaries; limitations on the volume of assets or number of service providers etc.)? What are the relevant market shares of foreign-owned financial institutions? • If there are controls on capital flows and foreign exchange, are they predictable and stable? • Are such restrictions reviewed periodically to assess their costs against the intended public purpose? • When the government owns or controls financial institutions in the country, what is the market share of the government-owned/controlled institutions? What is the perceived effect of government ownership in the sector? • Are there any specific restrictions on entry by domestic entities (e.g. requirements to serve certain geographic areas or market segments)? • (If relevant) Where policies have been adopted to support the development of Islamic banking, how does the government ensure an adequate level of competition in the sector and between Islamic and non-Islamic banking sectors?

Additional resources

Websites

OECD, *Financial Markets*, *www.oecd.org/finance/financial-markets/*.

OECD, *Insurance markets*, *www.oecd.org/finance/insurance/*.

OECD, *Bond Markets and Public Debt Management*, *www.oecd.org/finance/public-debt/local-currency-bond-markets.htm*.

OECD, *Pensions and Long-Term Investment Financing*, *www.oecd.org/finance/private-pensions/*.

Basel Committee on Banking Supervision, *www.bis.org/bcbs/index.htm*.

G20/OECD, Task Force on Institutional Investors and Long-Term Financing, *www.oecd.org/finance/principles-long-term-investment-financing-institutional-investors.htm*.

International Association of Insurance Supervisors, *http://iaisweb.org/index.cfm?event= showHomePage*.

International Organisation of Securities Commissions, *www.iosco.org/*.

USAID, Financial Sector Knowledge Sharing, *http://egateg.usaidallnet.gov/fsshare*.

World Bank, Financial Sector Development, *http://web.worldbank.org/WBSITE/EXTERNAL/TOPICS/EXTFINANCIALSECTOR/0,,menuPK:282892~pagePK:149018~piPK:149093~theSitePK: 282885,00.html*.

OECD instruments and tools

G20/OECD (2014), *Checklist on Long-Term Investment Financing Strategies and Institutional Investors*, OECD Paris, *www.oecd.org/daf/fin/private-pensions/G20-OECD%20Checklist%20on%20Long-term%20Investment%20Financing%20Strategies.pdf*.

G20/OECD (2013), *High-Level Principles for Long-Term Investment Financing by Institutional Investors*, OECD Paris, *www.oecd.org/daf/fin/private-pensions/G20-OECD-Principles-LTI-Financing.pdf*.

G20/OECD (2011), *High-Level Principles on Financial Consumer Protection*, OECD Paris, *www.oecd.org/daf/fin/financial-markets/48892010.pdf*.

OECD (2011), *OECD Guidelines on Insurer Governance*, OECD Publishing, Paris, *http://dx.doi.org/10.1787/9789264129320-en*.

OECD (2010), *Policy Framework for Effective and Efficient Financial Regulation and High-Level Checklist*, OECD Paris, *www.oecd.org/finance/financial-markets/44362818.pdf*.

OECD (2009), *Good Practices on Financial Education and Awareness Relating to Credit*, OECD Paris, *www.oecd.org/daf/fin/financial-education/46193051.pdf*.

OECD (2009), *OECD Recommendation on Core Principles of Occupational Pension Regulation*, OECD Paris, *www.oecd.org/pensions/private-pensions/33619987.pdf*.

OECD (2004), *OECD Principles of Corporate Governance*, OECD Paris, *www.oecd.org/daf/ca/corporate governanceprinciples/31557724.pdf*.

OECD/IMF/EBRD/World Bank (2013), *Local Currency Bond Markets: A Diagnostic Framework*. *www.imf.org/external/np/pp/eng/2013/070913.pdf*.

OECD/INFE (2012), *High-Level Principles on National Strategies for Financial Education*, OECD Paris, *www.oecd.org/finance/financial-education/OECD_INFE_High_Level_Principles_National_Strategies_Financial_Education_APEC.pdf*.

References, tools, guidance, manuals

ADB-OECD (2014), *ADB-OECD Study on Enhancing Financial Accessibility for SMEs*, OECD Publishing, Paris, *www.adb.org/sites/default/files/publication/41747/adb-oecd-study-enhancing-financial-accessibility-smes.pdf*.

IMF (1999), *Code of Good Practices on Transparency in Monetary and Financial Policies: Declaration of Principles*, IMF, Washington, DC, *www.imf.org/external/np/mae/mft/code/eng/code2e.pdf*.

OECD (2014), *Financing SMEs and Entrepreneurs 2014: an OECD Scoreboard*, OECD Publishing, Paris, *http://dx.doi.org/10.1787/fin_sme_ent-2014-en*.

World Bank (2014), *Global Financial Development Report 2014: Financial Inclusion,* The World Bank: Washington, DC, *http://siteresources.worldbank.org/EXTGLOBALFINREPORT/Resources/8816096-1361888425203/9062080-1364927957721/GFDR-2014_Complete_Report.pdf.*

World Bank-IMF (2005), Handbook on Financial Sector Assessment, The World Bank: Washington, DC, *https://openknowledge.worldbank.org/bitstream/handle/10986/7259/337970rev0Fina10Assessment01PUBLIC1.pdf?sequence=1.*

Statistics and indicators

OECD, *Corporate Governance Factbook 2014, www.oecd.org/daf/ca/CorporateGovernance Factbook.pdf.*

OECD, *FDI Regulatory Restrictiveness Index, www.oecd.org/investment/fdiindex.htm.*

OECD Financial Statistics, *Finance, http://stats.oecd.org/.*

IMF Financial Soundness Indicators, *http://data.imf.org/?sk=9F855EAE-C765-405E-9C9A-A9DC2C1FEE47.*

World Bank Indicators on Financial Inclusion and Infrastructure, *www.worldbank.org/en/topic/financial inclusion.*

Policy Framework for Investment
2015 Edition

11. Public governance

Regulatory policy is about the process by which regulations are drafted, updated, implemented and enforced. Regulations which encourage market dynamism, innovation and competitiveness improve economic performance. The aim of regulatory reform is to increase efficiency and effectiveness and to have a better balance in delivering social and economic policies over time. Key governance aspects considered here include quality regulation, transparency, and openness and integrity. Effective action across these dimensions will encourage investment and reduce the costs of doing business. Other, more general, aspects are considered in the *Horizontal Policies and Practices* section.

The quality of regulation has a significant influence on the climate for business and investment. Poorly designed or weakly applied regulations can slow business responsiveness, divert resources away from productive investments, hamper entry into markets, reduce job creation and generally discourage entrepreneurship. Nothing contributes more to investor confidence about regulation than predictability and the recognition that rules achieve their objectives. The quality of public services, which is shaped by regulation inside government as well as regulation for private sector providers, significantly influences the investment climate. From an investor's perspective, regulatory policy should provide strong guidance and benchmarks for action by officials and set out what investors can expect from government regarding regulation.

Regulatory framework

As markets become more open and interlinked, the need for well-designed regulatory frameworks and institutions is likely to rise, but the challenges facing regulators will also increase. From the perspective of investors, the important feature of regulatory quality is that it should have clear objectives and frameworks for implementation to ensure that, if regulation is used, the economic, social and environmental benefits justify the costs, the distributional effects are considered and the net benefits are maximised. Regulatory policy should set out principles providing strong guidance and benchmarks for action by officials, and defining clearly what investors can expect from government regarding regulation. In the past, regulation has often been sectorally driven and sometimes poorly coordinated across government departments, making the regulatory landscape complex. The move to a more comprehensive approach, frequently managed at the centre of government, helps to reduce the likelihood of contradictory or duplicative regulation and also helps to clarify the contribution of regulations in different policy fields to a defined overall objective such as competitiveness or red tape reduction. The OECD *Recommendation of the Council on Regulatory Policy and Governance* (2012) provides a detailed framework for defining an integrated, whole-of-government regulatory policy.

Administrative simplification

Administrative simplification aims to reduce and streamline government formalities and paperwork – the most visible component of which is often permits and licences – and thereby has a direct impact on the cost and efficiency of investing. In many countries, the administrative burden imposed on businesses is significant, particularly for small- to medium-sized enterprises. The informal economy often reflects administrative burdens that businesses, especially small firms, cannot meet. The right level of regulation, including attention to compliance costs when regulations are designed (through regulatory impact assessment), can help remove incentives for informal economic activity, with benefits for government, workers and investors. It is also important to consider the cumulative effect of all regulations, not just those that have been introduced recently. Increasingly, governments are making use of information and communication technologies to reduce administrative burdens and "red tape". Excessive "red tape" adds to business costs, can impede market entry, lowers competitive pressures (also see the section on *Competition Policy*) and reduces the incentive to innovate. It also creates uncertainty that can disrupt business planning and hinder the ability of businesses to respond quickly to new market opportunities. Ultimately, this discourages new domestic and foreign investment and weakens economic performance.

As part of the ongoing effort to reduce regulatory burdens and streamline regulation, systematic programme reviews of the stock of significant regulation should be conducted with clearly defined aims, including consideration of costs and benefits, to ensure that regulations remain up to date, cost justified, cost effective and consistent, and deliver the intended policy outcomes.

Regulatory impact assessments

Regulatory impact assessment (RIA) examines and measures the likely benefits, costs and effects of new or changed regulations. It provides decision makers with quantitative data and a framework for assessing their options and the likely economic, social and environmental consequences of their decisions. A poor understanding of the problems at hand or of the side effects of government action can undermine regulatory efforts and result in unintended consequences and regulatory failures. RIA is used to clearly identify problems for government action and to ensure that it is justified and appropriate in economic, social and environmental terms. The RIA process provides a systematic approach for assessing the impacts of a proposed regulation and helps inform regulatory decision-making. It offers a potentially useful tool for considering the impacts of regulation on investment decisions and may help identify and avoid regulations that impose unnecessary restrictions or that deter investment. The 2009 OECD *Introductory Handbook for Undertaking Regulatory Impact Analysis* outlines the key steps in developing a RIA-based approach to designing regulation. As many governments face the challenge of regaining or maintaining public trust and of delivering more and higher quality services with fewer resources, RIA should as far as possible be made publicly available along with regulatory proposals. Good practice would involve using RIA as part of the consultation process.

Regulatory compliance and enforcement

Governments should ensure that mechanisms and institutions are in place to enforce regulations and promote compliance. Inadequate and uneven enforcement tend to undermine the predictability of the regulatory framework for investors. In principle, regulations should be enforced in an equal manner for all economic actors. Too little attention has traditionally been paid to examining possibilities for improving the way regulations are implemented and enforced. A regulation cannot be effective without a proper enforcement mechanism. Inspections are one of the most important ways to enforce regulations and to ensure regulatory compliance. Good inspection planning, targeting and communication should be clearly integrated into the overall regulatory governance system, along with preventing corruption and promoting ethical behaviour. The 2014 OECD *Best Practice Principles in Regulatory Policy: Regulatory Enforcement and Inspections* provide a framework to support initiatives on improving regulatory enforcement through inspections, making them more effective, efficient and less burdensome for those who are inspected and, at the same time, less costly for governments. The principles address the design of the policies, institutions and tools to promote effective compliance – and the process of reforming inspection services to achieve results.

Governance and institutional structure

Independent regulators are playing an increasingly important role in delivering economic and societal objectives as well as being tasked with regulating more complex situations in a number of sectors, including utility sectors. Their activity has an important impact on economic regulation in the sectors that they oversee and helps to influence the capital investment, revenue flows and the returns on investment that investors can expect. Regulatory agencies also play a critical role in engaging with citizens and businesses on regulatory decisions. The state should develop a consistent policy covering the role and functions of regulatory agencies and the coordination mechanisms with relevant bodies to provide confidence that regulatory decisions are made on an objective, impartial and consistent basis, without conflict of interest, bias or improper influence. Regulatory agencies should be encouraged to work with stakeholders to manage the effective functioning of the market while also acting as a fair referee among market actors, in the interests of consumers. There should be systems for the review of the legality and procedural fairness of regulations and of the decisions made by agencies empowered to issue regulatory sanctions to ensure transparency and promote trust. These systems should be easily accessible to business and civil society at a reasonable cost. The OECD *Best Practice Principles for the Governance of Regulators* can help policy makers frame the governance arrangements of regulators to meet these objectives.

Regulatory coherence across levels of government and jurisdictions

The world is becoming increasingly global, providing great opportunities for investors that are reflected in growing international investment flows and the economic activity of multinationals, but the world is not "flat". Different country-specific norms and rules apply in different parts of the world. While specific rules and norms may cater for specific preferences, these divergences may sometimes raise unnecessary costs for businesses. The need for regulatory coherence across levels of government and at the international level is becoming particularly important for businesses that operate across borders. Where appropriate, regulatory coherence should be promoted through co-ordination mechanisms between supranational, national and sub-national levels of government. The benefits of high-quality regulation at one level of government might be undermined or even eliminated by low-quality regulation at lower levels of government. To eliminate unnecessary regulatory divergences that create additional burdens on investors and to address global challenges pertaining to systemic risks, the environment, and human health and safety, governments need to better articulate regulations across borders and to ensure greater application and enforcement of rules across jurisdictions. To provide guidance to countries on how to ensure coordination between national and international standard and regulations, the OECD has developed a typology of international regulatory co-operation mechanisms and is working on a specific guidance document (forthcoming, *Best-Practice Principles on International Regulatory Co-operation)*.

Open government

The shift to open government provides an important incentive for the public administration to enhance its performance. Both citizens and businesses are more able to examine the outcomes from public policy, comment on poor performance and encourage the government to improve. Over time, this is becoming an important force for reform and modernisation in the public sector. Citizen engagement is moving well beyond simple service delivery and consultation into joint implementation and citizen monitoring. Through web-based platforms and user-friendly data and information tools, governments can promote an "ecosystem" of diverse actors engaged in public policy implementation and the evaluation of outcomes. Open and inclusive policy making can improve policy performance by helping governments to better understand people's evolving needs and leverage the information, ideas and resources held by businesses. The OECD *Principles on Digital Governance* recognise that today's technology can support effective policies and create more open, transparent, innovative, participatory and trustworthy governments. However, many governments still do not see technology as a collaborative means to shape public governance outcomes. The main concern of the *Principles* is to promote a fundamental shift from citizen-centric approaches (government anticipating the needs of citizens and businesses) to citizen-driven approaches (citizens and businesses formulating and determining their needs in partnership with governments).

Translating this concept into practice remains a challenge. Governments need to invest in order to embed open and inclusive policy making as part of their "core business", to build skills among civil servants and to establish a supportive political and administrative culture. Evaluating the quality of open and inclusive policy making processes and their impacts is a new frontier for most governments. The updated *Guiding Principles for Open and Inclusive Policy Making* include ten recommendations to support government action. For example: rights to information, consultation and public participation in policy making and service delivery must be firmly grounded in law or policy. Government obligations to respond to citizens must be clearly stated. Independent oversight arrangements are essential for enforcing these rights. Adequate financial, human and technical resources are needed for effective public information, consultation and participation. Government officials must have access to appropriate skills, guidance and training as well as an organisational culture that supports both traditional and online tools. These guidelines provide a simple framework for countries to assess their efforts to become more open.

Public integrity

Integrity is a crucial determinant of a favourable investment climate. Comparative evidence suggests a link between trust in politicians, both from the business community and citizens, and the perception of corruption. Integrity tools and mechanisms, aimed at preventing corruption and fostering high standards of behaviour, help to reinforce the credibility and legitimacy of decision-making. Policy tools addressing high-risk areas at the intersection of the public and private sectors, including effective management of conflict of interest and adequate lobbying and political finance regulation, can be leveraged to limit policy capture and build safeguards to protect the public interest.

An effective policy approach to dealing with conflict of interest is essential to the political, administrative and legal structure of public life. The OECD *Guidelines for Managing Conflict of Interest in the Public Sector* provide a modern approach to conflict-of-interest policy that seeks to strike a balance by:

- Identifying risks to the integrity of public organisations and public officials;
- Prohibiting specific unacceptable forms of private interest;
- Making public organisations and individual officials aware of the circumstances in which conflicts can arise;
- Ensuring that effective procedures are deployed for identifying, disclosing, managing, and promoting the appropriate resolution of conflict-of-interest situations.

Box 11.1. **OECD country experience in managing conflicts of interest**

The majority of OECD countries have policies to manage conflict of interest, according to the OECD *Survey on Conflict of Interest* (2012). At the institutional level, 76% of OECD countries have a central function responsible for developing and maintaining conflict-of-interest policies, rules or procedures. Great importance is placed in most OECD countries on raising awareness and understanding of the policies surrounding potential conflict of interest. For example, in 97% of OECD countries, the conflict of interest policy is disseminated to public officials taking office or when they take on a new post. Some limitations remain. While disclosure of private interests by public officials is a common practice, information is only partially made available to the public in the majority of the OECD countries. This is in part due to the importance assigned to privacy concerns. Regarding effective implementation, only 24% of OECD countries employ diagnostic tools, such as surveys, statistical data, and cost-benefit analysis, to monitor the effective management of conflict of interest. Measuring compliance also remains a challenge, and while in the majority of OECD countries sanctions are foreseen in the event of a conflict-of-interest violation, no data exist on how sanctions are applied.

Source: OECD Survey on Conflict of Interest (2012).

The "revolving door" phenomenon, involving an increased movement of staff between the public and private sectors, has also raised concerns over pre- and post-public employment conditions and its negative effects on trust in the public sector. Such issues of impropriety (i.e. the misuse of "insider information", position and contacts) have led more and more countries to modernise arrangements to effectively prevent and manage conflict of interest in pre- and post-public employment. To balance conflicting interests, many countries have established standards or principles in order to ensure integrity in current or post-public officials. For example, a "cooling-off" period exists in many countries, where public servants must limit their interaction with their former organisation for a given length of time. The OECD *Post-Public Employment Principles* and *the Post-Public Employment Good Practice Framework* can act as a reference points for policy-makers to gauge their current or future post-public employment frameworks.

Private interests seeking to influence government decisions, legislation or the award of contracts through lobbying is part of the policy-making processes in modern democracies. Lobbying can contribute to good decision making and improve governments' understanding of policy issues by providing valuable insights and data as part of open consultation processes, but it can also lead to unfair advantages for vocal, specific interests when the process lacks transparency and accountability. The OECD *Principles for Transparency and Integrity in Lobbying* (2010) provide guidance to decision makers on promoting good governance in lobbying.

Public procurement

Public procurement is an important economic and government activity. It involves significant funds and is used to deliver public services to citizens as well as to achieve policy goals such as job creation, the development of small and medium enterprises (SMEs), environmental sustainability or innovation. Public procurement represents an average of 30% of general government expenditure and 13% of gross domestic product (GDP) in OECD Members, which translates to approximately € 4.3 trillion in 2012. Over half of total general government procurement spending across OECD Members is carried out at sub-national levels (55% on average).

Furthermore, public procurement is a high-risk area due to the close interaction between private and public spheres and because fraud, corruption and waste in procurement undermine the ability of government to serve its citizens properly. For these reasons, it is important to achieve high levels of efficiency, effectiveness and economy as well as to implement mechanisms to ensure the integrity and accountability of the procurement process. Doing so will prevent misuse of funds and help to reinforce citizens' trust in government. It is also important to safeguard the strategic role of public procurement through sound planning, design and delivery. An effective public procurement system serves the public's needs, provides customer satisfaction, delivers value for money in a fair, open, competitive and transparent way, ensuring a level playing field for all companies, and is regularly measured and evaluated for improvement.

The OECD *Recommendation on Public Procurement* reaffirms the role of public procurement as a strategic function. The *Recommendation* provides clear and effective guidance on how to implement a public procurement system that uses state-of-the-art tools and techniques to apply public funds sustainably and efficiently. At the same time, it will be an effective tool to address the challenges that are present in the governance of large investment projects such as public works, complicated digital technology systems, or major events.

Implementing international anti-corruption and integrity standards in national legislation

Anti-corruption and integrity standards include both preventive and repressive measures. Governments should enact provisions, mostly in criminal law, but also in the civil and administrative regulations, to prevent and sanction corruption of domestic public officials. Governments should also promote modern anti-corruption measures and encourage companies to invest in compliance systems in order to level the playing field in the fight against corruption.

Over the past decade, many governments have developed standards of conduct to address conflicts between public officials' private interests and their public duties.

Governments originally focused on traditional sources of influence, such as gifts or hospitality offered to public officials, and personal or family relationships. Due to the increased co-operation between the public and private sectors, many countries have also established in recent years standards of conduct for tackling other forms of conflict-of-interest, such as business interests (e.g. in the form of partnerships, shareholdings), affiliations with other organisations and post-public employment. In order to address risks to good governance arising from conflicts of interest, the OECD has developed a framework for reviewing and modernising a country's conflict-of-interest policy with the 2003 *Guidelines for Managing Conflict of Interest in the Public Service*, as well as a Toolkit to help public officials put them into practice.

Application and enforcement of anti-corruption laws and regulations

Application and enforcement of laws and regulations on anti-corruption and integrity involves many public institutions, and the laws need to be applied by independent law enforcement authorities free of political influence. Agency specific guidelines and practical measures (e.g. staff rotation, specific training or briefing) may need to be developed to enforce anti-corruption and integrity standards in parts of the public service that are particularly exposed to corruption. Specific risk areas include law enforcement, public procurement, export credit, development assistance as well as customs and tax administration.

Codes of conduct are often developed to provide standards of conduct in a single concise document. These should be made available and adequately communicated to all public officials. Socialisation mechanisms such as training and counselling further raise awareness among employees and help develop their skills for meeting expected integrity standards in daily practice. In addition, human resource management policies should provide suitable conditions and incentives for public officials, such as basing recruitment and promotion on merit, providing an adequate remuneration and taking ethical considerations into account in recruitment and performance appraisal.

Reporting suspicion of misconduct by public officials can be either required by law or facilitated by organisational rules. Whistle blowing, the act of raising concerns about misconduct within an organisation, is a key element of good governance to ensure transparency and accountability. A range of institutions and procedures such as Ombudsman, Inspector General, complaint procedures and help desks or telephone lines could enable public officials and citizens to expose wrongdoing. Their effectiveness also depends on public confidence that people who make bona fide reports about wrongdoing receive proper protection against retaliation.

Fighting corruption and other related misconduct can only be effective and sustainable if the public and the private sector join forces. This requires as a first step enhanced dialogue between public authorities and representatives of the private sector to determine joint measures and initiatives.

Review mechanisms for assessing anti-corruption performance

Solid and independent review is essential to help ensure enforcement of laws and regulations on anti-corruption and integrity. In general, the legislative branch undertakes reviews of public service activities. Other common types of evaluation range from external independent investigation by the Ombudsman or the Inspector General to specific judicial or ethics reviews. Monitoring compliance may be based on internal controls, widely used to detect individual irregularities and systemic failures, and is likely to be accompanied by independent scrutiny. This scrutiny keeps public officials accountable for their actions, ultimately, to the public.

Transparency in government operations is considered both as an instrument for ensuring accountability and combating corruption and for promoting democratic participation by informing and involving citizens. In recent years, public access to official information has significantly improved, particularly with the development of Freedom of Information legislation and the growing use of electronic procedures. Coupled with an increasingly active media and well-organised interest groups, this has led to more vigilant public scrutiny over public officials' behaviour.

International anti-corruption initiatives

Corruption cannot be addressed at the domestic level alone. Only concerted, internationally coordinated action can contribute meaningfully to stamping out corruption. Governments have consequently adopted a number of international and regional anti-corruption instruments. Although these instruments may have different focuses, they are complementary and reinforce one another, and thus aim at ensuring a holistic approach that encompasses preventive measures as well as repressive provisions to fight domestic and foreign corruption. Moreover, they contain provisions regarding mutual legal assistance, which facilitate detecting, investigating and sanctioning corruption.

There is also a role for international co-operation in the fight against corruption. For example, the OECD *Convention on Combating Bribery of Foreign Public Officials in International Business Transactions* aims to stop the flow of bribes to public officials in host countries. Other intergovernmental organisations such as the United Nations, the World Bank, the Asian Development Bank and the International Monetary Fund have likewise developed policies aimed at fostering good governance and sanctioning corruption and related malpractices. The OECD has also provided a framework to the G20 on developing common practices in the protection of whistleblowing.

Core questions and principles

Regulatory framework

1. Has the government established institutions and tools to ensure the quality and coherence of regulatory processes (e.g. the design, oversight and enforcement of rules in all sectors)?
2. What government procedures exist to identify and to reduce unnecessary regulatory burdens, including those on investors?
3. To what extent are regulatory impact assessments used to evaluate the consequences of regulations on the investment environment?
4. Are the necessary mechanisms in place to ensure regulatory compliance and enforcement and monitor regulatory outcomes?
5. Does the governance and institutional structure of regulators support an efficient and enabling regulatory environment?
6. What mechanisms are in place for ensuring regulatory coherence across levels of government, the transparent application of regulations, and clear standards for regulatory quality?

Public integrity

7. How does the government identify risks to the integrity of public organisations and public officials?
8. Is the public procurement system designed to assure proper access, competition and transparency while achieving efficiency and value? Has the government analysed the adequate alternatives and implications of pursuing investment projects through the different available solutions?
9. To what extent have international anti-corruption and integrity standards been implemented in national legislation and regulations? Do penal, administrative and civil law provisions provide an effective legislative and regulatory framework for fighting corruption and promoting integrity, thereby reducing uncertainty and improving business conditions for all investors?
10. Do institutions and procedures ensure transparent, effective and consistent application and enforcement of laws and regulations on anti-corruption and integrity in the public service?

Supplemental questions

Regulatory framework	• Has the government defined an integrated, whole-of-government policy for regulatory quality? • Does the policy have clear objectives and frameworks for implementation to ensure that the economic, social and environmental benefits of the regulation justify the costs, and that the distributional effects are considered and the net benefits maximised? • What mechanisms and institutions are in place to actively provide oversight of regulatory policy procedures and goals? • What mechanisms and institutions are in place to support and implement regulatory policy?
Administrative simplification	• To what extent are the administrative and other regulatory burdens on investors measured and quantified? • Does the government systematically review of the stock of significant regulation against clearly defined policy goals, including consideration of costs and benefits, to ensure that regulations are up to date, cost justified, cost effective and consistent, and that they deliver the intended policy objectives? • How does the government act upon the results of these reviews and the measures of administrative and other regulatory burdens on investors? • How does the government make use of information and communication technologies to reduce administrative burdens and red tape, and to streamline regulation?
Regulatory impact assessments	• Are regulatory impact assessments integrated into the early stages of the policy process for the formulation of new regulatory proposals? • Do they clearly identify policy goals, and evaluate if regulation is necessary and how it can be most effective and efficient in achieving those goals? • Do they consider means other than regulation and identify the trade-offs of the different approaches, in order to identify the best one? • Are the results of regulatory impact assessments made public on a timely basis?
Regulatory compliance and enforcement	• How does the design of policies, institutions and tools integrate enforcement and the promotion of effective compliance? • How are inspection planning, targeting and communication integrated into the overall regulatory governance system?
Governance and institutional structure	• How does policy on regulatory agencies' role, functions and coordination with other actors and stakeholders ensure that regulatory decisions are made on an objective, impartial and consistent basis, without conflict of interest, bias or improper influence? • What systems are in place to review the legality and procedural fairness of regulations and regulatory sanctions? Can business and civil society access these systems at a reasonable cost? • Are there regular reports on the performance of regulatory policy and reform programmes, the public authorities applying the regulations, and the functioning of regulatory tools (e.g. RIAs, public consultations, reviews of existing regulations)?
Regulatory coherence across levels of government and jurisdictions	• What mechanisms are in place to promote co-ordination between the supranational, the national and sub-national levels of government? • How does the government identify cross-cutting regulatory issues at all of these levels? • How is regulatory management capacity and performance developed, including at sub-national levels of government?

Open government	• What systems are used to ensure that regulation serves the public interest and is informed by the legitimate needs of those interested in and affected by regulation? • In order to ensure that concerned parties easily understand their rights and obligations, are regulations drafted to be comprehensible and clear? • Are the financial, human and technical resources adequate to guarantee effective public information? • Does the government provide opportunities for fair and equitable public participation in policy making and service delivery? • Are citizens' rights to information, prior consultation and public participation in policy making inscribed in law or policy? • Are there independent oversight arrangements on the enforcement of these rights?
Public integrity	• Is there a conflict of Interest policy, supported by organisational strategies and practices to help identify conflict of interest situations? • What procedures have been established for identifying, managing and resolving conflict of interest situations? • Has the government prohibited specific unacceptable forms of private interest? • How does the government create awareness among public organisations and individual officials of the circumstances in which conflicts can arise? • What procedures are in place for identifying, disclosing, managing, and promoting the appropriate resolution of conflict-of-interest situations? • How does the government ensure adequate transparency and accountability of lobbying? • How do rules and guidelines on lobbying address the governance concerns related to lobbying practices, and do they respect the socio-political and administrative contexts, including the wider policy and regulatory frameworks? • Are civil society organisations and the media free to scrutinise the conduct of public officials' duties? • Are "whistle-blower" protections in place to enable public officials and citizens to expose wrongdoing and report suspicion of misconduct by public officials? • Are these rules and guidelines reviewed on a periodic basis, and adjusted as necessary?
Public procurement	• What mechanisms are in place for the regular measurement, evaluation and improvement of the public procurement system to ensure its efficiency and value provision? • How does the government guarantee a level playing field and transparency in public procurement processes?
Application, enforcement and review of anti-corruption laws and regulations	• Have standards of conduct by public officials been established and made transparent? Are they made available and adequately communicated and transmitted to all public officials? • What measures are used to assist public officials and to ensure the expected standards are met with respect to conflict of interest, lobbying, revolving doors and other high risk issues? • Are there agency-specific guidelines and practical measures (e.g. staff rotation, specific training or briefing etc.) to enforce anti-corruption and integrity standards in parts of the public service that are particularly exposed to corruption? • Do review mechanisms exist to assess the performance of laws and regulations on anti-corruption and integrity? • Does the government encourage the private sector to put in place effective compliance systems? • Does the government promote a dialogue between the public and private sector on how to fight corruption and related misconduct? • How are review mechanisms to assess the performance of laws and regulations on anti-corruption and integrity used to improve these laws and regulations?
International anti-corruption and integrity standards and initiatives	• Is the government a party to international initiatives aimed at fighting corruption and improving public sector integrity? • Do the international initiatives aimed at fighting corruption and improving public sector integrity review the government's level of implementation of the relevant international standards? • Are reviews of the government's level of implementation of the international standards on fighting corruption and improving public sector integrity published? • Has the government effectively implemented recommendations from these initiatives?

Additional resources

OECD, *Public governance*, *www.oecd.org/governance/*.

IMF (1998), "Roads to Nowhere: How Corruption in Public Investment Hurts Growth", *Economic Issues* 12, IMF.

OECD (2015 forthcoming), *Regulatory Policy Outlook 2015*, OECD Publishing, Paris.

OECD (2014), *Regulatory Enforcement and Inspections*, OECD Best Practice Principles for Regulatory Policy, OECD Publishing, Paris, *http://dx.doi.org/10.1787/9789264208117-en*.

OECD (2014), *Best Practice Principles in Regulatory Policy: The Governance of Regulators*, OECD Paris, *www.oecd.org/gov/regulatory-policy/governance-regulators.htm*.

OECD (2013), *International Regulatory Co-operation: Addressing Global Challenges*, OECD Publishing, Paris, *http://dx.doi.org/10.1787/9789264200463-en*.

OECD (2012), *Recommendation of the Council on Regulatory Policy and Governance*, *www.oecd.org/governance/regulatory-policy/49990817.pdf*.

OECD (2010), "Implementing the Post-Public Employment Principles: A good practice framework", in OECD, *Post-Public Employment: Good Practices for Preventing Conflict of Interest*, OECD Publishing, Paris, *http://dx.doi.org/10.1787/9789264056701-7-en*.

OECD (2010), *OECD Principles for Transparency and Integrity in Lobbying*, OECD, Paris, *www.oecd.org/gov/ethics/oecdprinciplesfortransparencyandintegrityinlobbying.htm*.

OECD (2009), *Focus on Citizens: Public Engagement for Better Policy and Services*, OECD Studies on Public Engagement, OECD Publishing, Paris, *http://dx.doi.org/10.1787/9789264048874-en*.

OECD (2005), *Managing Conflict of Interest in the Public Sector: A Toolkit*, OECD Publishing, Paris, *http://dx.doi.org/10.1787/9789264018242-en*.

OECD (1997), *OECD Convention on Combatting Bribery of Foreign Public Officials in International Business Transactions*, OECD, Paris, *www.oecd.org/corruption/oecdantibribery convention.htm*.

United Nations (2005), *United Nations Convention against Corruption*.

United Nations Global Programme against Corruption, United Nations Office for Drug Control and Crime Prevention, UNODCCP, *www.unodc.org/unodc/corruption/*.

World Bank, Public Sector Governance Programme.

Policy Framework for Investment
2015 Edition

12. Investment framework for green growth

Investment for green growth needs to be scaled-up significantly to support the path to sustainable development and to achieve economic, development, social and environmental policy goals. Achieving sustainable development includes staying below the two-degree* (2°C) climate change goal agreed by governments, adapting to the impacts of climate change, reducing pollution, promoting biodiversity conservation and sustainable use, and ensuring that the benefits of ecosystem services are universally available. Green growth means "fostering economic growth and development while ensuring that natural assets continue to provide the resources and environmental services on which our well-being relies". To do this, an economy must support a growth dynamic that catalyses investment and innovation in new technologies, services and infrastructure that will underpin growth that makes a more sustainable claim on natural resources while addressing poverty reduction and social equity considerations (OECD, 2011a). Beyond efforts to mainstream green growth considerations in investment in general, this section focuses on opportunities for scaling-up "green investment". Green investment notably includes investment in:

- Green infrastructure and greening of existing infrastructure (e.g. in sustainable energy, energy and resource efficiency, sustainable transport, buildings, water sanitation and distribution systems and waste management, enabling infrastructure like smart grids and interconnectors, and climate-resilient infrastructure including retrofitting existing infrastructure);
- Sustainable management of natural resources management and the services they provide (e.g. fisheries, forests, wildlife and nature-based tourism, soil productivity, water security and minerals); and
- Activities within the environmental goods and services sector, and across entire segments of green value chains (e.g. traditional upstream or midstream industries producing intermediate inputs for solar photovoltaic or wind-energy manufacturing among others) and greening of existing value chains.

These three types of green investment share many characteristics, but are ultimately distinct in nature. The investment vehicles used to achieve each will typically differ greatly, as will the most relevant barriers to investment. The policy tools used to foster or govern them may also differ.

* At the 2012 United Nations Framework Convention on Climate Change (UNFCCC) Conference of the Parties in Doha, governments decided to "urgently work towards the deep reduction in global greenhouse gas emissions required to hold the increase in global average temperature below 2 °C above pre-industrial levels and to attain a global peaking of global greenhouse gas emissions as soon as possible".

Given the scale of investment needs, mobilising and scaling-up green investments implies leveraging domestic and international, public and private investment. Often, however, green infrastructure projects remain seriously constrained by specific investment barriers. Key policy obstacles include notably: weak or non-existent pricing of negative externalities; subsidies that promote inefficient resource use; an erratic policy and regulatory environment; market and regulatory rigidities that favour the incumbency of existing polluting technologies; a lack of mechanisms to capture the value of ecosystem services for sustainable natural resource management; and an entire range of distortions affecting water infrastructure. In addition to removing barriers, governments can support private investment for green growth by establishing a predictable policy and regulatory environment for green investment. Governments can mitigate regulatory risk by providing greater certainty for investors through transparency and comprehensive consultations with private sector on policy reforms and drafting of laws and regulations. They can also mobilise private finance through domestic and international public interventions (e.g. ensuring that international public finance can leverage private finance or facilitating private sector participation in green infrastructure).

A policy framework for green investment is in many respects comparable to an enabling environment that is conducive to investment in general. Policies conducive only to investment, however, will not automatically result in a substantial increase of green investment. A policy framework for investment is thus a necessary but insufficient condition for green growth and green investment. Policy makers will also need to improve specific enabling conditions for green investment by developing policies and regulations that systematically internalise the cost of negative externalities (e.g. by putting a price on carbon, setting congestion charges in cities, or developing financial regulations that recognise and reward environmental and social performance). Pricing environmental externalities needs to be done in a credible way, while taking into account national circumstances and potential competitiveness impacts. Designing green investment policies would also require using environmental valuation techniques to ensure that government cost-benefit analysis takes into account the cost associated with the depleted natural resources and environmental degradation. The policy framework will need to send a coherent signal to investors, producers and consumers to demonstrate the value of a green versus brown pathway for future growth and development.

Green investment creates opportunities for economies at different stages of development, such as: improving energy security by reducing reliance on fossil-fuel imports; reducing local air pollution and associated health costs; and stimulating innovation and technology transfer. Developing economies can also “leapfrog” older technologies to avoid locking-in carbon-intensive development pathways, while meeting rising demand for infrastructure investment in a more cost-effective way. Investment for green growth can also contribute to creating value and employment across different segments of value chains. Governments have a key role to play in designing green investment incentive schemes to maximise these benefits, and internalise the costs of environmental externalities, as well as the benefits of green investment. Business can also play an important role in green investment through various means, including: creating awareness of risks and opportunities; supporting consumers to reduce their environmental impact; improving others’ performance through supply chains; making transparent and informed decisions; and collaborating in leading sustainable solutions that can be used across multiple industries.

Recent years have seen a resurgence of interest in targeted policies to attract investment in particular segments of green value chains, as opposed to policies that aim to improve the investment climate across the board. In the post-crisis recovery context, several governments have designed "green industrial policies" aimed at supporting domestic production of environmental goods and services. They have done so notably through establishing local-content requirements, as well as trade-distorting subsidies. In a context of global value chains, however, such policies can hinder international green investment and competitiveness, by raising the cost of inputs for downstream activities (OECD, 2015c). This is particularly critical for small developing countries with low domestic demand and relatively poor supporting infrastructure. Unless they target activities where there is potential to eventually compete on world markets (a difficult criterion to assess *ex ante*), policies of this type could increase the costs of domestically purchased environmental goods. In addition, domestic support measures that discriminate among various kinds of investors are not mutually supportive and might result in sub-optimal investment flows at global level.

This section does not follow a one-size-fits-all approach. Countries need to devise their own strategies for green investment, which need to be tailored to their specific circumstances, needs and priorities. Ways of promoting green investment depend on policy and institutional settings, levels of development, natural resource environmental pressure points, as well as political will and leadership to set priorities. Despite the unique circumstances of every country, a number of common considerations need to be addressed in all settings.

This section aims to assist governments in identifying those common elements to help mobilise investment for green growth. Key issues for policy makers' consideration include:

- Ensuring strong government commitment at both the international and national levels to support green growth and catalyse private green investment;
- Improving the coherence of investment promotion and facilitation measures, including to align the broad system of investment incentives and disincentives and phase out inefficient fossil-fuel subsidies to support green growth as a means to sustainable development;
- Reforming policies to enable green investment, including by applying essential investment policy principles such as non-discrimination, transparency and property protection in areas susceptible to attract green investment, e.g. in renewable energy, water resources management or multi-modal, climate-resilient transport infrastructure systems;
- Addressing market and regulatory rigidities that favour incumbent fossil-fuel and resource intensive technologies and practices, for instance in the transport, electricity or water sectors (see section on *Competition Policy*);
- Providing public financial tools, instruments and funds to facilitate access to financing and attract co-financing for green projects including to attract long-term institutional investment, while ensuring value for public money;
- Enhancing co-ordination and improving public governance across and within levels of government, especially among environment and natural resource management, energy and investment authorities;
- Establishing policies to encourage environmentally responsible business conduct and broad stakeholder participation in green growth including in green investment strategies; and
- Addressing other cross-cutting issues, such as: setting policies to support effective private sector participation (whether international or domestic) in green infrastructure projects, including through joint ventures or public-private partnerships (PPPs); and addressing outstanding barriers to international trade and investment in environmental goods, services and projects.

Core questions and principles

1. What are the country's green growth priorities and objectives and how are they reflected in: national vision or goals for development; development, land use or infrastructure plans; and policies particularly with respect to infrastructure investment and land-use?
2. What policies, laws, market-based instruments and regulations (including sector-specific ones) are in place to encourage private investment in support of green growth, while contributing to other policy agendas such as poverty reduction?
3. Has the government provided transitional support to green investment and uptake of green technologies and practices, for instance through well-targeted and time-limited investment incentives, innovation, innovative financing or reformed financial regulations to incentivise green investment?
4. Does the government respect core investment principles such as investor protection, intellectual property rights protection and non-discrimination in areas susceptible to attract green investment?
5. Do the competition laws and their application ensure a level playing field between incumbents and new entrants in green infrastructure markets?
6. How does the government ensure consistency and coherence of environmental, sectoral, economic and investment policies that affect private green investment across and within different levels of government and public agencies?
7. What steps has the government taken to align national and sub-national (including urban-level) policies that could have an impact on green investment?
8. Is there a clearly defined legal framework for public procurement, PPPs and other co-financing arrangements in support of green investment?
9. How does the government consult with the private sector and other local stakeholders in the design and implementation of strategies and plans, policies and regulations that are relevant for green investment? What is the role of science and technology policies and research and development (R&D) institutions in promoting green investment?
10. Is the government addressing outstanding barriers to international trade and ensuring that green investment policies are compatible with WTO rules? How can international trade rules be used to promote such policies?

Supplemental questions

Overview of green investment opportunities	• What is the country's general resource endowment (natural resources, biodiversity, energy mix, etc.)? • What are the country's international commitments in support of green growth, e.g. greenhouse gas (GHG) emission reduction targets under the United Nations Framework Convention on Climate Change (UNFCCC), or biodiversity-related engagements under the Convention on Biological Diversity (CBD)? • What natural resource constraints or scarcity risks exist (or may arise in the future) that may constrain future development? • What does the country consider to be its main challenges and opportunities for green growth across the different segments of green value chains? What does the government perceive to be the main barriers to green investment? Has the country identified the investment needs to achieve its green growth objectives? • Does the government adequately balance the need to meet both environmental and investment policy objectives? • Has the government identified priorities to increase the country's participation in global green value chains, across the various segments (including downstream infrastructure projects, midstream manufacturing and upstream raw material extraction)? • Is the government considering the contribution of green growth and green investment opportunities to poverty reduction, social equity and social inclusion policy goals?

Government's commitment towards green growth	• Does the country include environmental and natural resource endowment considerations in its infrastructure and/or national development plans? If so how and if not, does it plan to do so and how? • Are there policies or legislation in place that deal with private investment in the area(s) identified as priorities for green growth? (e.g. in renewable energies, energy efficiency, reforestation and/or water)? • Which ministries and agencies are involved in developing and co-ordinating investment policies designed to support of green growth? What are their respective roles? • Do international investment agreements (IIA) and free trade agreements (FTAs), to which the country is a party, take into account environmental issues? If so, please specify which ones and how.
Investment promotion and facilitation: key policies and incentives for green investment	• Has the government taken measures to remove inefficient fossil-fuel subsidies? Are the level and efficiency of these subsidies monitored on a regular basis? • Has the government put in place pricing mechanisms, such as taxes on carbon or other emissions or land-value taxes, to support green growth? What other measures are in place to address market failures, e.g. those relevant notably to green infrastructure or land use sectors? • Has the government used emission trading schemes such as the Clean Development Mechanism (CDM) to achieve its climate change goals or to stimulate the development national, sub-national and regional emissions trading systems? • What incentives (e.g. subsidies, tax exemptions and feed-in tariffs) are in place to stimulate private investment in support of green growth goals? • Are incentives time-limited and appropriately targeted? (see section on *Tax Policy* for tailored guidance on tax incentives) • Does the government adequately monitor and assess the objectives, costs and success of policy measures in support of green investment and what types of benchmarks for success are in place, if any? • On environmental effectiveness and monitoring: How does the government assess and monitor the costs and environmental effectiveness of taxes, subsidies and other incentives for green investment (ex-ante and ex-post)? • What steps is the government taking to make green investment policies part of a broader national infrastructure, energy, land-use planning, environment and climate strategy framework? • What steps has the government taken to promote linkages between green businesses, especially between foreign affiliates and local enterprises? (see the section on *Investment Promotion and Facilitation* for an in-depth treatment of investment linkages) • What measures has the government put in place to address the specific challenges faced by SMEs to invest in green growth? • Is the government considering the distributional impacts of green investment incentives and disincentives (e.g. associating fossil-fuel subsidy reforms with cash transfers)? • As markets for new green technologies mature, is the government ensuring that the targets of transitional policy incentive measures evolve to keep targeting technologies that are not yet competitive, and to avoid inefficient subsidies? • Is the government ensuring that short-run policy support is flexible and technology-neutral, to avoid locking green sectors into inefficient and outdated infrastructure and technologies? • How is the government assessing the cost-effectiveness of policy support to green technologies and activities within the green value chains?
Investment policy and enabling policies for green investment	• Does the government ensure that laws and regulations governing green investment are non-discriminatory across different types of investors, whether public or private, foreign or domestic? • What steps is the government taking to protect intellectual property rights for green technologies? Are laws and regulations for the protection of intellectual property rights for green technologies effectively enforced? What steps is the government taking to facilitate environmental innovation in green sectors and other sectors? • Is the system of contract enforcement effective and widely accessible to all investors in green infrastructure? • What steps is the government taking to facilitate the business licensing process for green projects? • Is the government addressing green protectionist measures (such as local content requirements) that are increasingly being challenged in investor-state dispute settlement (ISDS) and international treaty claims? At the same time, is the government monitoring whether investment treaties are interfering with environmental policies?
Competition issues with regards to green investment	• Have the competition authorities adequately addressed anti-competitive practices by incumbent enterprises, including state-owned enterprises (SOE), which inhibit green investment and hinder green growth? • Do private investors and producers benefit from non-discriminatory access to finance for green investment? • Are SOEs and private companies competing on a level playing field on the energy markets? Has separation, whether accounting, functional or structural, between generation, transmission and distribution of renewable energy been considered as a solution to facilitate investment by independent power producers (IPPs)?
Financial market policy and financial instruments	• What financial instruments and mechanisms (e.g. risk-mitigation and return-enhancement mechanisms, preferential loans, green bonds, public environmental funds or green funds by private banks) are in place to stimulate private investment in support of green growth, including to attract long-term institutional investment? • How do existing public finance institutions (e.g. national development banks, green investment banks, etc) seek to mobilise and scale up investment financing from the private sector? • What financial regulations (i.e. well-functioning insurance markets that cover against natural catastrophes) are in place that may incentivise investment to provide green growth benefits? Has the governments given due consideration to unintended consequences which financial regulations could have on green investment?

Public governance	• What mechanisms are in place for managing regulatory reform across different levels of government to ensure consistent and transparent application of regulations and policies designed to promote green growth, and clear standards for regulatory quality? (e.g. steering committees, roundtables, issuance of environmental licenses etc.) • What steps is the government taking to ensure the independence of regulators (e.g. for electricity markets)? • Are environmental and green growth considerations such as long-term climate change impacts and climate resilience accounted in public procurement of infrastructure projects such as roads, and into national and sub-national infrastructure planning? • Has the government fully integrated green infrastructure planning with land-use planning? • Has the government integrated green growth consideration in urban land-use planning and zoning policies (e.g. to discourage urban sprawl or avoid new infrastructure facilities to be located in flood-prone areas)? • Do public procurement policies include environmental and green growth considerations such as resource-efficiency, pollution abatement and climate resilience? How are these criteria communicated to potential providers?
Promoting green business conduct and stakeholder participation in green growth	• What environmental impact assessment and strategic environmental assessment requirements are in place and are they adequately enforced? • What measures has the government taken to promote "green" responsible business conduct (e.g. reporting of corporate environmental information, application of environmental management systems, training of staff in environmental issues, information to consumers, certification and labelling, etc.)? • How is the government consulting with other civil society groups and encouraging public (including consumers') awareness of and engagement with green growth objectives? • What measures are in place to promote skills development (in both the public and private sectors) and prepare the labour force in areas relevant to green investment?
Regional co-operation	• Has the government made use of international and regional initiatives aimed at building expertise to promote green investment? • What steps is the government taking towards the regional integration of national and sub-national infrastructure markets?
Making and implementing the choice of public and private provision for green growth	• Is the government considering using public-private partnerships (PPPs) to mobilise private sector funding and/or expertise in the development and management of green infrastructure? Is the government considering other types of public-private collaboration for green areas? • What are the institutional, regulatory and legislative conditions, tools and provisions in place to ensure the financial sustainability, accountability and "value for money" of green PPP projects (e.g. administrative capacity within the relevant government institutions, competitive bidding processes, output-based contracts, dispute resolution mechanisms, ex ante estimation of projects' affordability, transparency and full disclosure of conditions in biddings, or creation of PPP units)? • Are PPP contracts designed to allow appropriate risk-sharing and flexibility? • Are environmental performance criteria built into PPPs?
Trade policy	• How actively is the government increasing green investment opportunities through trade agreements and through the implementation of its WTO commitments?
Biodiversity, water and natural resource management	• Does the government price natural resources to provide a stable economic incentive for green investment (e.g. investing more in water infrastructure and in environmentally-sound treatment of natural resources)? • Does the government use innovative financial mechanisms for scaling-up finance and investment for biodiversity, such as Payments for Ecosystem Services (PES), environmental fiscal reform or biodiversity offsets?

Additional resources

Websites

OECD, *Financing climate change action*, *www.oecd.org/env/cc/financing.htm*.

OECD, *Green growth and sustainable development*, *www.oecd.org/greengrowth*.

OECD, *Investment for green growth*, *www.oecd.org/investment/green.htm*.

Tools, guidance, manuals

Ang, G. and V. Marchal (2013), "Mobilising Private Investment in Sustainable Transport: The Case of Land-Based Passenger Transport Infrastructure", *OECD Environment Working Papers*, No. 56, OECD Publishing, Paris, *http://dx.doi.org/10.1787/5k46hjm8jpmv-en*.

Corfee-Morlot, J. et al. (2012), "Towards a Green Investment Policy Framework: The Case of Low-Carbon, Climate-Resilient Infrastructure", *OECD Environment Working Papers*, No. 48, OECD Publishing, Paris, *http://dx.doi.org/10.1787/5k8zth7s6s6d-en*.

Gordon, K. and J. Pohl (2011), "Environmental Concerns in International Investment Agreements: A Survey", *OECD Working Papers on International Investment*, No. 2011/01, OECD Publishing, Paris, *http://dx.doi.org/10.1787/5kg9mq7scrjh-en*.

G20/OECD (2012), "Policy Note on Pension Fund Financing for Green Infrastructure and Initiatives."

IEA (2014), *Energy Technology Perspectives 2014*, IEA, Paris, *http://dx.doi.org/10.1787/energy_ tech-2014-en*.

IEA (2012), *Energy Technology Perspectives 2012: Pathways to a Clean Energy System*, OECD Publishing, Paris, *http://dx.doi.org/10.1787/energy_tech-2012-en*.

IEA, OPEC, OECD and World Bank (2011), "Joint report by IEA, OPEC, OECD and World Bank on fossil-fuel and other energy subsidies: An update of the G20 Pittsburgh and Toronto Commitments", Prepared for the G20 Meeting of Finance Ministers and Central Bank Governors and the G20 Summit, 2011.

Kaminker, C. et al. (2013), "Institutional Investors and Green Infrastructure Investments: Selected Case Studies", *OECD Working Papers on Finance, Insurance and Private Pensions*, No. 35, OECD Publishing, Paris, *http://dx.doi.org/10.1787/5k3xr8k6jb0n-en*.

Kaminker, C. and F. Stewart (2012), "The Role of Institutional Investors in Financing Clean Energy", *OECD Working Papers on Finance, Insurance and Private Pensions*, No. 23, OECD Publishing, Paris, *http://dx.doi.org/10.1787/5k9312v21l6f-en*.

OECD (2015, forthcoming), *Aligning Policies for the Transition to a Low-Carbon Economy*, OECD Publishing, Paris.

OECD (2015a), *Mapping Channels to Mobilise Institutional Investment in Sustainable Energy*, Green Finance and Investment, OECD Publishing, Paris, *http://dx.doi.org/10.1787/9789264224582-en*.

OECD (2015b), *Policy Guidance for Investment in Clean Energy Infrastructure: Expanding Access to Clean Energy for Green Growth and Development*, OECD Publishing, Paris, *http://dx.doi.org/10.1787/9789264212664-en*.

OECD (2015c), *Overcoming Barriers to International Investment in Clean Energy*, OECD Publishing, Paris.

OECD (2013a), "How to unlock private investment in support of green growth?", Issue Note prepared for the Green Growth and Sustainable Development Forum 2013, 5-6 December, 2013, Paris.

OECD (2013b), "Enabling Investment in Sustainable Energy Infrastructure", OECD Post-2015 Series.

OECD (2011a), *Towards Green Growth*, OECD Green Growth Studies, OECD Publishing, Paris, *http://dx.doi.org/10.1787/9789264111318-en*.

OECD (2011b), "Annex 1. Harnessing freedom of investment for green growth", in OECD, *Towards Green Growth*, OECD Publishing, Paris, *http://dx.doi.org/10.1787/9789264111318-8-en*.

OECD (2010), *Transition to a Low-Carbon Economy: Public Goals and Corporate Practices*, OECD Publishing, Paris, *http://dx.doi.org/10.1787/9789264090231-en*.

OECD (2009), *Private Sector Participation in Water Infrastructure: OECD Checklist for Public Action*, OECD Studies on Water, OECD Publishing, Paris, *http://dx.doi.org/10.1787/9789264059221-en*.

OECD (2006), *Recommendation of the Council on Good Practices for Public Environmental Expenditure Management*, OECD Publishing, Paris.

Reviews, case/country studies and indicators

Francke, E. et al. (2012), "The Mobilisation of Private Investment for Low-carbon, Climate-Resilient Infrastructure: The Case of Metrobus Bus Rapid Transit System in Mexico City", case study prepared by CTS EMBARQ Mexico for the OECD.

OECD (2015 forthcoming), *Inventory of Estimated Budgetary Support and Tax Expenditures for Fossil Fuels 2015*, OECD Publishing, Paris.

OECD (2014), *Green Growth Indicators 2014*, OECD Green Growth Studies, OECD Publishing, Paris, *http://dx.doi.org/10.1787/9789264202030-en*.

OECD (2013c), *OECD Investment Policy Reviews: Malaysia 2013*, OECD Publishing, Paris, *http://dx.doi.org/10.1787/9789264194588-en*.

OECD (2013d), *OECD Investment Policy Reviews: Costa Rica 2013*, OECD Publishing, Paris, *http://dx.doi.org/10.1787/9789264203952-en*.

OECD (2013e), *OECD Investment Policy Reviews: Jordan 2013*, OECD Publishing, Paris, *http://dx.doi.org/10.1787/9789264202276-en*.

OECD (2013f), *Inventory of Estimated Budgetary Support and Tax Expenditures for Fossil Fuels 2013*, OECD Publishing, Paris, *http://dx.doi.org/10.1787/9789264187610-en*.

OECD (2012a), *OECD Investment Policy Reviews: Tunisia 2012*, OECD Publishing, Paris, *http://dx.doi.org/10.1787/9789264179172-en*.

OECD (2012b), *OECD Investment Policy Reviews: Colombia 2012*, OECD Publishing, Paris, *http://dx.doi.org/10.1787/9789264167742-en*.

ORGANISATION FOR ECONOMIC CO-OPERATION AND DEVELOPMENT

The OECD is a unique forum where governments work together to address the economic, social and environmental challenges of globalisation. The OECD is also at the forefront of efforts to understand and to help governments respond to new developments and concerns, such as corporate governance, the information economy and the challenges of an ageing population. The Organisation provides a setting where governments can compare policy experiences, seek answers to common problems, identify good practice and work to co-ordinate domestic and international policies.

The OECD member countries are: Australia, Austria, Belgium, Canada, Chile, the Czech Republic, Denmark, Estonia, Finland, France, Germany, Greece, Hungary, Iceland, Ireland, Israel, Italy, Japan, Korea, Luxembourg, Mexico, the Netherlands, New Zealand, Norway, Poland, Portugal, the Slovak Republic, Slovenia, Spain, Sweden, Switzerland, Turkey, the United Kingdom and the United States. The European Commission takes part in the work of the OECD.

OECD Publishing disseminates widely the results of the Organisation's statistics gathering and research on economic, social and environmental issues, as well as the conventions, guidelines and standards agreed by its members.

ÉDITIONS OCDE, 2, rue André-Pascal, 75775 PARIS CEDEX 16
(20 2014 04 1 P) ISBN 978-92-64-20865-0 – 2015-18

www.ingramcontent.com/pod-product-compliance
Lightning Source LLC
Chambersburg PA
CBHW061219240926
51846CB00006B/1284
* 9 7 8 9 2 6 4 2 0 8 6 5 0 *